COLLEGE

WITHDRAWN

D1087968

THE GOSPEL ACCORDING TO THOMAS

THE GOSPEL
ACCORDING TO THOMAS

COPTIC TEXT ESTABLISHED AND TRANSLATED

BY

A. GUILLAUMONT, H.-CH. PUECH, G. QUISPEL,
W. TILL AND † YASSAH 'ABD AL MASĪḤ

H|B

LEIDEN
E. J. BRILL

NEW YORK
HARPER & BROTHERS

COPYRIGHT © E. J. BRILL 1959

PRINTED IN THE UNITED STATES OF AMERICA

All rights reserved, including television, radio broadcasting, dramatic and motion-picture rights, and the right of published edition in the Coptic text. No part of this book may be reproduced or translated in any form by print, photoprint, microfilm, or any other means without written permission from the publisher.

229.8
B582t

PRELIMINARY REMARKS

What follows is nothing more than a fragment of a work which is much more extensive and complete: a critical, scholarly edition of *The Gospel according to Thomas*, which will include a long introduction devoted to the various problems—philological, historical and exegetical—which have been raised by the document, as well as the Coptic text of the writing, a translation in German, French or English, a commentary consisting of detailed notes, and an index of Coptic and Greek terms. This volume will be published in the near future. In view, however, of certain technical difficulties which have delayed the printing and publication of the larger work, we think it wise to make available in advance this extract. *The Gospel according to Thomas* is a document so important, the announcement of its discovery and what has already been said concerning it have evoked so great a curiosity on the part of the general public and so great an interest on the part of the scholarly world, that it is impossible for us to delay its publication further or to decide otherwise.

By extracting this section of the coming edition and by publishing it beforehand, we have intended above all to furnish a preliminary working tool for purposes of instruction and research, so that our colleagues may proceed on the solid ground provided by the text itself, here transcribed and occasionally reconstructed, and may more easily judge its translation, which has been made as literal as possible.

The numerals which appear at the top and in the margin of the left-hand pages refer to the plates of the photographic edition of the manuscript, which we owe to Dr. Pahor Labib

9860

(*Coptic Gnostic Papyri in the Coptic Museum at Old Cairo*, vol. I, Cairo 1956, pl. 80, line 10-pl. 99, line 28). The numerals which appear at the top of the right-hand pages, or have been inserted within parentheses on these pages, correspond to the numbers of the 114 *logia*, which represent our enumeration within this collection of "Sayings of Jesus", which comprise almost exclusively the present "Gospel".

The critical apparatus and the notes refer only to the constitution and the primary interpretation of the text. A summary list of scriptural parallels or echoes has been added in the form of an appendix. The variants, the extra-canonical parallels, the testimonies of the indirect tradition relative to this or that *logion*, the Semitisms which here or there lie beneath the surface, and other analogies, will be expounded in the commentary of the authoritative edition.

The manuscript, now preserved in the Coptic Museum of Old Cairo, has been collated there, in October 1956, by three of us. It belongs to one of the thirteen volumes which together form the Gnostic library found, about 1945, in the neighborhood of Nag-Hamâdi (Upper Egypt); this volume is Codex III of our classification. The Codex must probably be dated either in the second half of the Fourth Century A.D. or in the beginning of the Fifth Century A.D. But the original of *The Gospel according to Thomas*—the second of the seven writings contained in this volume—goes back much earlier. We are dealing here with a translation or an adaptation in Sahidic Coptic of a work the primitive text of which must have been produced in Greek about 140 A.D., and which was based on even more ancient sources.

The English text of this edition has been read by Paul S. Minear of Yale University Divinity School.

For further details see:

H.-Ch. Puech, Une collection de Paroles de Jésus récemment retrouvée: L'Évangile selon Thomas, in *Comptes Rendus de l'Académie des Inscriptions et Belles-Lettres* (Institut de France), 1957, pp. 146-167.

H.-Ch. Puech, Das Thomas-Evangelium, in E. Hennecke-W. Schneemelcher, *Neutestamentliche Apokryphen*[3], t. I, Tübingen, 1959, pp. 199-223.

G. Quispel, The Gospel of Thomas and the New Testament, in *Vigiliae Christianae*, XI, 1957, pp. 189-207.

G. Quispel, L'Évangile selon Thomas et les Clémentines, *ibid.*, XII, 1958, pp. 181-196.

A. Guillaumont, Sémitismes dans les logia de Jésus retrouvés à Nag-Hamâdi, in *Journal Asiatique*, CCXLVI, 1958, pp. 113-123.

W. C. Till, New Sayings of Jesus in the Recently Discovered Coptic, "Gospel of Thomas", in *Bulletin of the John Rylands Library* XLI, 1959, pp. 446-458.

THE GOSPEL ACCORDING TO THOMAS

80 10 ναει νε ⲛ̅ϣⲁϫⲉ ⲉⲑⲏⲡ' ⲉⲛⲧⲁⲓⲥ ⲉⲧⲟⲛϩ·
ϫⲟⲟⲩ ⲁⲩⲱ ⲁϥⲥϩⲁⲓ̈ⲥⲟⲩ ⲛ̅ϭⲓ ⲇⲓⲇⲩⲙⲟⲥ

12 ⲓ̈ⲟⲩⲇⲁⲥ ⲑⲱⲙⲁⲥ (1) ⲁⲩⲱ ⲡⲉϫⲁϥ ϫⲉ ⲡⲉ
ⲧⲁϩⲉ ⲉⲑⲉⲣⲙⲏⲛⲉⲓⲁ ⲛ̅ⲛⲉⲉⲓϣⲁϫⲉ ϥⲛⲁ

14 ϫⲓ †ⲡⲉ ⲁⲛ ⲙ̅ⲡⲙⲟⲩ· (2) ⲡⲉϫⲉ ⲓ̅ⲥ̅ ⲙ̅ⲛ̅ⲧⲣⲉϥ'
ⲗⲟ ⲛ̅ϭⲓ ⲡⲉⲧ'ϣⲓⲛⲉ ⲉϥ'ϣⲓⲛⲉ ϣⲁⲛⲧⲉϥ'

16 ϭⲓⲛⲉ ⲁⲩⲱ ϩⲟⲧⲁⲛ' ⲉϥϣⲁⲛϭⲓⲛⲉ ϥⲛⲁ
ϣⲧⲣⲧⲣ ⲁⲩⲱ ⲉϥϣⲁⲛϣⲧⲟⲣⲧⲣ ϥⲛⲁⲣ

18   (blank)   ϣⲡⲏⲣⲉ ⲁⲩⲱ ϥⲛⲁⲣ
ⲣ̅ⲣⲟ ⲉϫⲙ̅ ⲡⲧⲏⲣϥ (3) ⲡⲉϫⲉ ⲓ̅ⲥ̅ ϫⲉ ⲉⲩϣⲁ

20 ϫⲟⲟⲥ ⲛⲏⲧⲛ̅ ⲛ̅ϭⲓ ⲛⲉⲧ'ⲥⲱⲕ ϩⲏⲧ' ⲧⲏⲩⲧⲛ̅
ϫⲉ ⲉⲓⲥ ϩⲏⲏⲧⲉ ⲉⲧ'ⲙ̅ⲛⲧⲉⲣⲟ ϩⲛ̅ ⲧⲡⲉ ⲉ

22 ⲉⲓⲉ ⲛ̅ϩⲁⲗⲏⲧ' ⲛⲁⲣ̅ ϣⲟⲣⲡ' ⲉⲣⲱⲧⲛ̅ ⲛⲧⲉ
ⲧⲡⲉ ⲉⲩϣⲁⲛϫⲟⲟⲥ ⲛⲏⲧⲛ̅ ϫⲉ ⲥ̅ϩⲛ̅ ⲑⲁ

24 ⲗⲁⲥⲥⲁ ⲉⲉⲓⲉ ⲛ̅ⲧⲃ̅ⲧ' ⲛⲁⲣ̅ ϣⲟⲣⲡ' ⲉⲣⲱⲧⲛ̅
ⲁⲗⲗⲁ ⲧⲙ̅ⲛⲧⲉⲣⲟ ⲥ̅ⲙ̅ⲡⲉⲧⲛ̅ϩⲟⲩⲛ' ⲁⲩⲱ

26 ⲥ̅ⲙ̅ⲡⲉⲧⲛ̅ⲃⲁⲗ' ϩⲟⲧⲁⲛ ⲉⲧⲉⲧⲛ̅ϣⲁⲛ
ⲥⲟⲩⲱⲛ ⲧⲏⲩⲧⲛ̅ ⲧⲟⲧⲉ ⲥⲉⲛⲁⲥⲟⲩⲱ

81 ⲧⲏⲛⲉ ⲁⲩⲱ ⲧⲉⲧⲛⲁⲉⲓⲙⲉ ϫⲉ ⲛ̅ⲧⲱⲧⲛ̅ ⲡⲉ

2 ⲛ̅ϣⲏⲣⲉ ⲙ̅ⲡⲉⲓⲱⲧ' ⲉⲧⲟⲛϩ ⲉϣⲱⲡⲉ ⲇⲉ
ⲧⲉⲧⲛⲁⲥⲟⲩⲱⲛ ⲧⲏⲩⲧⲛ̅ ⲁⲛ ⲉⲉⲓⲉ ⲧⲉⲧⲛ̅

4 ϣⲟⲟⲡ' ϩⲛ̅ ⲟⲩⲙⲛ̅ⲧϩⲏⲕⲉ ⲁⲩⲱ ⲛ̅ⲧⲱⲧⲛ̅
ⲡⲉ ⲧⲙ̅ⲛⲧϩⲏⲕⲉ (4) ⲡⲉϫⲉ ⲓ̅ⲥ̅ ϥⲛⲁϫⲛⲁⲩ ⲁⲛ

6 ⲛ̅ϭⲓ ⲡⲣⲱⲙⲉ ⲛ̅ϩⲗ̅ⲗⲟ ϩⲛ̅ ⲛⲉϥϩⲟⲟⲩ ⲉϫⲛⲉ
ⲟⲩⲕⲟⲩⲉⲓ ⲛ̅ϣⲏⲣⲉ ϣⲏⲙ ⲉϥϩⲛ̅ ⲥⲁϣϥ̅

8 ⲛ̅ϩⲟⲟⲩ ⲉⲧⲃⲉ ⲡⲧⲟⲡⲟⲥ ⲙ̅ⲡⲱⲛϩ ⲁⲩⲱ
ϥⲛⲁⲱⲛϩ ϫⲉ ⲟⲩⲛ̅ ϩⲁϩ ⲛ̅ϣⲟⲣⲡ' ⲛⲁⲣ̅ ϩⲁ

2

80 10 These are the secret words which the Living Jesus
spoke and Didymos Judas Thomas wrote.

12 (1) And He said :
Whoever finds the explanation (ἑρμηνεία) of these words will

14 not taste death. (2) Jesus said:
Let him who seeks, not cease seeking until he

16 finds, and when (ὅταν) he finds, he will
be troubled, and when he has been troubled, he will

18 marvel and he will
reign over the All. (3) Jesus said: If

20 those who lead you say to you:
"See, the Kingdom is in heaven",

22 then the birds of the heaven will precede you.
If they say to you: "It is in the sea (θάλασσα),"

24 then the fish will precede you.
But (ἀλλά) the Kingdom is within you and

26 it is without you. If (ὅταν) you (will)
know yourselves, then (τότε) you will be known

81 and you will know that you are

2 the sons of the Living Father. But (δέ) if
you do not know yourselves, then you

4 are in poverty and you
are poverty. (4) Jesus said: The man old in days will not

6 hesitate to ask
a little child of seven

8 days about the place (τόπος) of Life, and
he will live. For many who are first shall become last

10 ⲉ ⲁⲩⲱ ⲛ̄ⲥⲉϣⲱⲡⲉ ⲟⲩⲁ ⲟⲩⲱⲧ (5) ⲡⲉϫⲉ ⲓ̄ⲥ̄
ⲥⲟⲩⲱⲛ ⲡⲉⲧⲙ̄ⲡⲙ̄ⲧⲟ ⲙ̄ⲡⲉⲕϩⲟ ⲉⲃⲟⲗ`

12 ⲁⲩⲱ ⲡⲉⲑⲏⲡ` ⲉⲣⲟⲕ· ϥⲛⲁϭⲱⲗⲡ̄ ⲉⲃⲟⲗ
ⲛⲁⲕ· ⲙⲛ̄ ⲗⲁⲁⲩ ⲅⲁⲣ ⲉϥϩⲏⲡ· ⲉϥⲛⲁⲟⲩⲱⲛϩ

14 ⲉⲃⲟⲗ ⲁⲛ (6) ⲁⲩϫⲛⲟⲩϥ ⲛ̄ϭⲓ ⲛⲉϥ`ⲙⲁⲑⲏⲧⲏⲥ
ⲡⲉϫⲁⲩ ⲛⲁϥ ϫⲉ ⲕ`ⲟⲩⲱϣ ⲉⲧⲣⲛ̄ⲣⲛⲏⲥⲧⲉⲩⲉ

16 ⲁⲩⲱ ⲉϣ ⲧⲉ ⲑⲉ ⲉⲛⲁϣⲗⲏⲗ ⲉⲛⲁϯ ⲉⲗⲉ
ⲏⲙⲟⲥⲩⲛⲏ ⲁⲩⲱ ⲉⲛⲁⲣⲡⲁⲣⲁⲧⲏⲣⲉⲓ ⲉⲟⲩ

18 ⲛ̄ϭⲓⲟⲩⲱⲙ` ⲡⲉϫⲉ ⲓ̄ⲥ̄ ϫⲉ ⲙ̄ⲡⲣϫⲉ ϭⲟⲗ ⲁⲩ
ⲱ ⲡⲉⲧⲉⲧⲙ̄ⲙⲟⲥⲧⲉ ⲙ̄ⲙⲟϥ` ⲙ̄ⲡⲣⲁⲁϥ ϫⲉ

20 ⲥⲉϭⲟⲗⲡ̄· ⲧⲏⲣⲟⲩ ⲉⲃⲟⲗ ⲙ̄ⲡⲉⲙⲧⲟ ⲉⲃⲟⲗ
ⲛ̄ⲧⲡⲉ ⲙⲛ̄ ⲗⲁⲁⲩ ⲅⲁⲣ ⲉϥϩⲏⲡ· ⲉϥⲛⲁⲟⲩ

22 ⲱⲛϩ ⲉⲃⲟⲗ ⲁⲛ ⲁⲩⲱ ⲙⲛ̄ ⲗⲁⲁⲩ ⲉϥϩⲟⲃⲥ̄ ⲉⲩ
ⲛⲁϭⲱ ⲟⲩⲉϣⲛ̄ ϭⲟⲗⲡϥ` (7) ⲡⲉϫⲉ ⲓ̄ⲥ̄ ⲟⲩ

24 ⲙⲁⲕⲁⲣⲓⲟⲥ ⲡⲉ ⲡⲙⲟⲩⲉⲓ ⲡⲁⲉⲓ ⲉⲧⲉ
ⲡⲣⲱⲙⲉ ⲛⲁⲟⲩⲟⲙϥ ⲁⲩⲱ ⲛ̄ⲧⲉⲡⲙⲟⲩⲉⲓ

26 ϣⲱⲡⲉ ⲣ̄ⲣⲱⲙⲉ ⲁⲩⲱ ϥⲃⲏⲧ` ⲛ̄ϭⲓ ⲡⲣⲱ
ⲙⲉ ⲡⲁⲉⲓ ⲉⲧⲉ ⲡⲙⲟⲩⲉⲓ ⲛⲁⲟⲩⲟⲙϥ ⲁⲩ

28 ⲱ ⲡⲙⲟⲩⲉⲓ ⲛⲁϣⲱⲡⲉ ⲣ̄ⲣⲱⲙⲉ (8) ⲁⲩⲱ ⲡⲉ
ϫⲁϥ ϫⲉ ⲉⲡⲣⲱⲙⲉ ⲧⲏⲧⲱⲛ ⲁⲩⲟⲩⲱϩⲉ

30 ⲣ̄ⲣⲙⲛ̄ϩⲏⲧ` ⲡⲁⲉⲓ ⲛ̄ⲧⲁϩⲛⲟⲩϫⲉ ⲛ̄ⲧⲉϥⲁ
ⲃⲱ ⲉⲑⲁⲗⲁⲥⲥⲁ ⲁϥⲥⲱⲕ ⲙ̄ⲙⲟⲥ ⲉϩⲣⲁⲓ̈

32 ϩⲛ̄ ⲑⲁⲗⲁⲥⲥⲁ ⲉⲥⲙⲉϩ ⲛ̄ⲧⲃⲧ̄ ⲛ̄ⲕⲟⲩⲉⲓ ⲛ̄
ϩⲣⲁⲓ̈ ⲛ̄ϩⲏⲧⲟⲩ ⲁϥϩⲉ ⲁⲩⲛⲟϭ ⲛ̄ⲧⲃⲧ̄ ⲉⲛⲁ

21 ⲛ̄ⲧⲡⲉ *sic*; *l.* ⲛ̄ⲧⲙⲉ?
28 *sic*; *l.* ⲡⲣⲱⲙⲉ ⲛⲁϣⲱⲡⲉ ⲙ̄ⲙⲟⲩⲉⲓ

10 and they shall become a single one. (5) Jesus said:
Know what is in thy sight,

12 and what is hidden from thee will be revealed
to thee. For (γάρ) there is nothing hidden which will

14 not be manifest. (6) His disciples (μαθητής) asked Him,
they said to Him: Wouldst thou that we fast (νηστεύειν),

16 and how should we pray (and) should we give alms (ἐλεημοσύνη),
and what diet should we observe (παρατηρεῖν)?

18 Jesus said: Do not lie;
and do not do what you hate, for

20 all things are manifest before Heaven.
For (γάρ) there is nothing hidden that shall not

22 be revealed and there is nothing covered that
shall remain without being uncovered. (7) Jesus said:

24 Blessed (μακάριος) is the lion which
the man eats and the lion

26 will become man; and cursed is the man
whom the lion eats and

28 the lion will become man. (8) And He said:
The Man is like a wise fisherman

30 who cast his net
into the sea (θάλασσα), he drew it up

32 from the sea (θάλασσα) full of small fish;
among them he found a large (and) good fish,

11 "what" or "him who".
15 read: "How wouldst thou".
20 "Heaven": perhaps originally "the Truth".
28 read: "the man will become lion".

5

34 ноту' ⲛ̄ϭⲓ ⲡⲟⲩⲱⲣⲉ ⲣ̄ⲣⲙ̄ⲛ̄ϩⲏⲧ' ⲁϥⲛⲟⲩ

ⲍⲉ ⲛ̄ⲛⲕⲟⲧⲉⲓ ⲧⲏⲣⲟⲩ ⲛ̄ⲧⲃ̄ⲧ' ⲉⲃⲟⲗ ⲉ[ⲡⲉ]

82 ⲥⲏⲧ ⲉⲑⲁⲗⲁⲥⲥⲁ ⲁϥⲥⲱⲧⲡ̄· ⲙ̄ⲡⲛⲟϭ ⲛ̄

2 ⲧⲃ̄ⲧ ⲭⲱⲣⲓⲥ ϩⲓⲥⲉ ⲡⲉⲧⲉ ⲟⲩⲛ̄ ⲙⲁⲁⲍⲉ ⲙ̄ⲙⲟϥ

ⲉⲥⲱⲧⲙ̄ ⲙⲁⲣⲉϥ'ⲥⲱⲧⲙ̄ (9) ⲡⲉⲭⲉ ⲓ̄ⲥ̄ ⲍⲉ ⲉⲓⲥ ϩⲏ

4 ⲛ̄ⲧⲉ ⲁϥⲉⲓ ⲉⲃⲟⲗ ⲛ̄ϭⲓ ⲡⲉⲧ'ⲥⲓⲧⲉ ⲁϥⲙⲉϩ ⲧⲟⲟⲧϥ̄

ⲁϥⲛⲟⲩⲍⲉ ⲁϩⲟⲉⲓⲛⲉ ⲙⲉⲛ ϩⲉ ⲉⲍⲛ̄ ⲧⲉϩⲓⲏ'

6 ⲁⲩⲉⲓ ⲛ̄ϭⲓ ⲛ̄ϩⲁⲗⲁⲧⲉ ⲁⲩⲕⲁⲧϥⲟⲩ ϩⲛ̄ⲕⲟⲟⲧⲉ

ⲁⲩϩⲉ ⲉⲍⲛ̄ ⲧⲡⲉⲧⲣⲁ ⲁⲩⲱ ⲙ̄ⲡⲟⲩⲍⲉ ⲛⲟⲩⲛⲉ

8 ⲉⲡⲉⲥⲏⲧ' ⲉⲡⲕⲁϩ ⲁⲩⲱ ⲙ̄ⲡⲟⲩⲧⲉⲩⲉ ϩⲙ̄ⲥ ⲉϩ

ⲣⲁⲓ̈ ⲉⲧⲡⲉ ⲁⲩⲱ ϩⲛ̄ⲕⲟⲟⲧⲉ ⲁⲩϩⲉ ⲉⲍⲛ̄ ⲛ̄ϣⲟ

10 ⲧⲉ ⲁⲩⲱϭⲧ' ⲙ̄ⲡⲉϭⲣⲟϭ ⲁⲩⲱ ⲁⲡϥ̄ⲛⲧ ⲟⲩⲟⲙⲟⲩ

ⲁⲩⲱ ⲁϩⲛ̄ⲕⲟⲟⲩⲉ ϩⲉ ⲉⲍⲛ̄ ⲡⲕⲁϩ ⲉⲧⲛⲁⲛⲟⲩϥ'

12 ⲁⲩⲱ ⲁϥϯ ⲕⲁⲣⲡⲟⲥ ⲉϩⲣⲁⲓ̈ ⲉⲧⲡⲉ ⲉⲛⲁⲛⲟⲩϥ· ⲁϥ

ⲉⲓ ⲛ̄ⲥⲉ ⲉⲥⲟⲧⲉ ⲁⲩⲱ ϣⲉ ⲍⲟⲩⲱⲧ· ⲉⲥⲟⲧⲉ

14 (10) ⲡⲉⲭⲉ ⲓ̄ⲥ̄ ⲍⲉ ⲁⲉⲓⲛⲟⲩⲍⲉ ⲛ̄ⲟⲩⲕⲱϩⲧ' ⲉⲍⲛ̄

ⲡⲕⲟⲥⲙⲟⲥ ⲁⲩⲱ ⲉⲓⲥ ϩⲏⲏⲧⲉ ϯⲁⲣⲉϩ ⲉⲣⲟϥ'

16 ϣⲁⲛⲧⲉϥⲍⲉⲣⲟ (11) ⲡⲉⲭⲉ ⲓ̄ⲥ̄ ⲍⲉ ⲧⲉⲉⲓⲡⲉ ⲛⲁⲣⲡⲁ

ⲣⲁⲅⲉ ⲁⲩⲱ ⲧⲉⲧⲛ̄ⲧⲡⲉ ⲙ̄ⲙⲟⲥ ⲛⲁⲣ̄ⲡⲁⲣⲁⲅⲉ

18 ⲁⲩⲱ ⲛⲉⲧⲙⲟⲟⲩⲧ ⲥⲉⲟⲛϩ ⲁⲛ ⲁⲩⲱ ⲛⲉⲧⲟⲛϩ

ⲥⲉⲛⲁⲙⲟⲩ ⲁⲛ ⲛ̄ϩⲟⲟⲩ ⲛⲉⲧⲉⲧⲛ̄ⲟⲩⲱⲙ'

20 ⲙ̄ⲡⲉⲧⲙⲟⲟⲩⲧ' ⲛⲉⲧⲉⲧⲛ̄ⲉⲓⲣⲉ ⲙ̄ⲙⲟϥ ⲙ̄ⲡⲉ

ⲧⲟⲛϩ ϩⲟⲧⲁⲛ ⲉⲧⲉⲧⲛ̄ϣⲁⲛϣⲱⲡⲉ ϩⲙ̄ ⲡⲟⲩ

22 ⲟⲉⲓⲛ ⲟⲩ ⲡⲉⲧⲉⲧⲛ̄ⲁⲁϥ ϩⲙ̄ ⲫⲟⲟⲩ ⲉⲧⲉⲧⲛ̄

12/13 ⲁϥⲉⲓ for ⲁϥϥⲓ ?

14 ⲁⲉⲓⲛⲟⲩⲍⲉ perhaps for ⲁⲉⲓⲉⲓ ⲉⲛⲟⲩⲍⲉ ?

19 ⲛⲉⲧⲉⲧⲛ̄ *sic*; *l.* ⲉⲛⲉⲧⲉⲧⲛ̄

6

34 that wise fisherman, he threw
   all the small fish

32   down into the sea (θάλασσα), he chose the large

2 fish without (χωρίς) regret. Whoever has ears
   to hear let him hear. (9) Jesus said: See,

4 the sower went out, he filled his hand,
   he threw. Some (seeds) (μέν) fell on the road;

6 the birds came, they gathered them. Others
   fell on the rock (πέτρα) and did not strike root

8 in the earth and did not produce ears.
   And others fell on the thorns;

10 they choked the seed and the worm ate them.
   And others fell on the good earth;

12 and it brought forth good fruit (καρπός);
   it bore sixty per measure and one hundred twenty per measure.

14 (10) Jesus said: I have cast fire upon
   the world (κόσμος), and see, I guard it

16 until it (the world) is afire. (11) Jesus said: This heaven shall
   pass away (παράγειν) and the one above it shall pass away (παράγειν),

18 and the dead are not alive and the living
   shall not die. In the days when you devoured

20 the dead, you made it alive;
   when (ὅταν) you come into light,

22 what will you do? On the day when you

---

14 "I have cast"; read probably: "I have come to cast" (comp. p. 83, 32).

ⲟ ⲛ̄ⲟⲩⲁ ⲁⲧⲉⲧⲛ̄ⲉⲓⲣⲉ ⲙ̄ⲡⲥⲛⲁⲩ ϩⲟⲧⲁⲛ ⲇⲉ

24 ⲉⲧⲉⲧⲛ̄ϣⲁϣⲱⲡⲉ ⲛ̄ⲥⲛⲁⲩ ⲟⲩ ⲡⲉ ⲉⲧⲉ

ⲧⲛ̄ⲛⲁⲁϥ' (12) ⲡⲉϫⲉ ⲙ̄ⲙⲁⲑⲏⲧⲏⲥ ⲛ̄ⲓⲥ ϫⲉ ⲧⲛ̄

26 ⲥⲟⲟⲩⲛ ϫⲉ ⲕⲛⲁⲃⲱⲕ ⲛ̄ⲧⲟⲟⲧⲛ̄ ⲛⲓⲙ' ⲡⲉ

ⲉⲧⲛⲁⲣ̄ ⲛⲟϭ ⲉϩⲣⲁï ⲉϫⲱⲛ ⲡⲉϫⲉ ⲓ̅ⲥ̅ ⲛⲁⲩ

28 ϫⲉ ⲡⲙⲁ ⲛ̄ⲧⲁⲧⲉⲧⲛ̄ⲉⲓ ⲙ̄ⲙⲁⲩ ⲉⲧⲉⲧⲛⲁ

ⲃⲱⲕ' ϣⲁ ïⲁⲕⲱⲃⲟⲥ ⲡⲇⲓⲕⲁⲓⲟⲥ ⲡⲁⲉⲓ ⲛ̄ⲧⲁ

30 ⲧⲡⲉ ⲙⲛ̄ ⲡⲕⲁϩ ϣⲱⲡⲉ ⲉⲧⲃⲏⲧϥ̄ (13) ⲡⲉϫⲉ ⲓ̅ⲥ̅

ⲛ̄ⲛⲉϥⲙⲁⲑⲏⲧⲏⲥ ϫⲉ ⲧⲛ̄ⲧⲱⲛⲧ̄' ⲛ̄ⲧⲉⲧⲛ̄

32 ϫⲟⲟⲥ ⲛⲁⲉⲓ ϫⲉ ⲉⲉⲓⲛⲉ ⲛ̄ⲛⲓⲙ ⲡⲉϫⲁϥ ⲛⲁϥ

ⲛ̄ϭⲓ ⲥⲓⲙⲱⲛ ⲡⲉⲧⲣⲟⲥ ϫⲉ ⲉⲕⲉⲓⲛⲉ ⲛ̄ⲟⲩⲁⲅ'

34 ⲅⲉⲗⲟⲥ ⲛ̄ⲇⲓⲕⲁⲓⲟⲥ ⲡⲉϫⲁϥ ⲛⲁϥ ⲛ̄ϭⲓ ⲙⲁⲑ'

83 ⲑⲁⲓⲟⲥ ϫⲉ ⲉⲕⲉⲓⲛⲉ ⲛ̄ⲟⲩⲣⲱⲙⲉ ⲙ̄ⲫⲓⲗⲟⲥⲟ

2 ⲫⲟⲥ ⲛ̄ⲣⲙ̄ⲛ̄ϩⲏⲧ' ⲡⲉϫⲁϥ ⲛⲁϥ ⲛ̄ϭⲓ ⲑⲱⲙⲁⲥ

ϫⲉ ⲡⲥⲁϩ ϩⲟⲗⲱⲥ ⲧⲁⲧⲁⲡⲣⲟ ⲛⲁϣⲁⲡϥ' ⲁⲛ

4 ⲉⲧⲣⲁϫⲟⲟⲥ ϫⲉ ⲉⲕⲉⲓⲛⲉ ⲛ̄ⲛⲓⲙ' ⲡⲉϫⲉ ⲓⲏⲥ

ϫⲉ ⲁⲛⲟⲕ' ⲡⲉⲕ'ⲥⲁϩ ⲁⲛ ⲉⲡⲉⲓ ⲁⲕⲥⲱ ⲁⲕ†ϩⲉ

6 ⲉⲃⲟⲗ ϩⲛ̄ ⲧⲡⲏⲅⲏ ⲉⲧⲃ̄ⲣ̄ⲃⲣⲉ ⲧⲁⲉⲓ ⲁⲛⲟⲕ'

ⲛ̄ⲧⲁⲉⲓϣⲓⲧⲉ ⲁⲩⲱ ⲁϥϫⲓⲧϥ̄ ⲁϥⲁⲛⲁⲭⲱⲣⲉⲓ

8 ⲁϥϫⲱ ⲛⲁϥ ⲛ̄ϣⲟⲙⲧ̄' ⲛ̄ϣⲁϫⲉ ⲛ̄ⲧⲁⲣⲉ ⲑⲱ

ⲙⲁⲥ ⲇⲉ ⲉⲓ ϣⲁ ⲛⲉϥ'ϣⲃⲉⲉⲣ' ⲁⲩϫⲛⲟⲩϥ' ϫⲉ

10 ⲛ̄ⲧⲁ ⲓ̅ⲥ̅ ϫⲟⲟⲥ ϫⲉ ⲟⲩ ⲛⲁⲕ' ⲡⲉϫⲁϥ' ⲛⲁⲩ ⲛ̄ϭⲓ

ⲑⲱⲙⲁⲥ ϫⲉ ⲉⲓϣⲁⲛ'ϫⲱ ⲛⲏⲧⲛ̄ ⲟⲩⲁ ϩⲛ̄ ⲛ̄ϣⲁ

12 ϫⲉ ⲛ̄ⲧⲁϥϫⲟⲟⲩ ⲛⲁⲉⲓ ⲧⲉⲧⲛⲁϥⲓ ⲱⲛⲉ ⲛ̄ⲧⲉ

ⲧⲛ̄ⲛⲟⲩϫⲉ ⲉⲣⲟⲉⲓ ⲁⲩⲱ ⲛ̄ⲧⲉⲟⲩⲕⲱϩⲧ̄ ⲉⲓ ⲉ

32 ⲉⲉⲓⲛⲉ *sic; l.* ⲉⲓⲉⲓⲛⲉ

7 ϣⲓⲧⲉ perhaps for ϣⲁⲕⲧⲉ ?

8

were one, you became two. But (δέ) when (ὅταν)

24 you have become two, what will you do?

(12) The disciples (μαθητής) said to Jesus:

26 We know that thou wilt go away from us. Who is it
who shall be great over us? Jesus said to them:

28 Wherever you have come, you will
go to James the righteous (δίκαιος)

30 for whose sake heaven and earth came into being. (13) Jesus said
to His disciples (μαθητής): Make a comparison to Me and

32 tell Me whom I am like. Simon Peter
said to Him: Thou art like a

34 righteous (δίκαιος) angel (ἄγγελος). Matthew said to Him:

83 Thou art like a wise (φιλόσοφος) man of understanding.

2 Thomas said to Him:
Master, my mouth will not at all (ὅλως) be capable

4 of saying whom Thou art like. Jesus said:
I am not thy Master, because (ἐπεί) thou hast drunk, thou hast

6 from the bubbling spring (πηγή) which I   [become drunk
have measured out. And He took him, He withdrew (ἀναχωρεῖν),

8 He spoke three words to him.
Now (δέ) when Thomas came to his companions, they asked him:

10 What did Jesus say to thee? Thomas said to them:
If I tell you one of the words

12 which He said to me, you will take up stones and
throw at me; and fire will come from

---

7 "measured"; perhaps: "dug".

14 ⲃⲟⲗ ⲟⲛ ⲛ̄ⲱⲛⲉ ⲛ̄ⲥⲣⲱⲡⲕ̄ ⲙ̄ⲙⲱⲧⲛ̄ (14) ⲡⲉϫⲉ
ⲓ̅ⲥ̅ ⲛⲁⲩ ϫⲉ ⲉⲧⲉⲧⲛ̄ϣⲁⲛⲣⲛⲏⲥⲧⲉⲩⲉ ⲧⲉⲧⲛⲁ
16 ϫⲡⲟ ⲛⲏⲧⲛ̄ ⲛ̄ⲛⲟⲩⲛⲟⲃⲉ ⲁⲩⲱ ⲉⲧⲉⲧⲛ̄ϣⲁ
ϣⲗⲏⲗ ⲥⲉⲛⲁⲣ̄ⲕⲁⲧⲁⲕⲣⲓⲛⲉ ⲙ̄ⲙⲱⲧⲛ̄ ⲁⲩⲱ
18 ⲉⲧⲉⲧⲛ̄ϣⲁⲛϯ ⲉⲗⲉⲏⲙⲟⲥⲩⲛⲏ ⲉⲧⲉⲧⲛⲁⲉⲓ
ⲣⲉ ⲛⲟⲩⲕⲁⲕⲟⲛ ⲛ̄ⲛⲉⲧⲙ̄ⲡⲛ̄ⲁ ⲁⲩⲱ ⲉⲧⲉⲧⲛ̄
20 ϣⲁⲛⲃⲱⲕ̄ ⲉϩⲟⲩⲛ ⲉⲕⲁϩ ⲛⲓⲙ ⲁⲩⲱ ⲛ̄ⲧⲉⲧⲛ̄
ⲙⲟⲟϣⲉ ϩⲛ̄ ⲛ̄ⲭⲱⲣⲁ ⲉⲩϣⲁⲣⲡⲁⲣⲁⲇⲉⲭⲉ
22 ⲙ̄ⲙⲱⲧⲛ̄ ⲡⲉⲧⲟⲩⲛⲁⲕⲁⲁϥ ϩⲁⲣⲱⲧⲛ̄ ⲟⲩⲟⲙϥ
ⲛⲉⲧϣⲱⲛⲉ ⲛ̄ϩⲏⲧⲟⲩ ⲉⲣⲓ̈ⲑⲉⲣⲁⲡⲉⲩⲉ ⲙ̄ⲙⲟ
24 ⲟⲩ ⲡⲉⲧⲛⲁⲃⲱⲕ̄ ⲅⲁⲣ̄ ⲉϩⲟⲩⲛ ϩⲛ̄ ⲧⲉⲧⲛ̄ⲧⲁ
ⲡⲣⲟ ϥⲛⲁϫⲱϩⲙ̄ ⲧⲏⲩⲧⲛ̄ ⲁⲛ̄ ⲁⲗⲗⲁ ⲡⲉⲧⲛ̄
26 ⲛⲏⲩ ⲉⲃⲟⲗ ϩⲛ̄ ⲧⲉⲧⲛ̄ⲧⲁⲡⲣⲟ ⲛ̄ⲧⲟϥ ⲡⲉ
ⲧⲛⲁϫⲁϩⲙ̄ ⲧⲏⲩⲧⲛ̄ (15) ⲡⲉϫⲉ ⲓ̅ⲥ̅ ϫⲉ ϩⲟⲧⲁⲛ
28 ⲉⲧⲉⲧⲛ̄ϣⲁⲛⲛⲁⲩ ⲉⲡⲉⲧⲉ ⲙ̄ⲡⲟⲩϫⲡⲟϥ
ⲉⲃⲟⲗ ϩⲛ̄ ⲧⲥϩⲓⲙⲉ ⲡⲉϩⲧ̄ ⲧⲏⲩⲧⲛ̄ ⲉϫⲙ̄
30 ⲡⲉⲧⲛ̄ϩⲟ ⲛ̄ⲧⲉⲧⲛ̄ⲟⲩⲱϣⲧ ⲛⲁϥ ⲡⲉⲧⲙ̄
ⲙⲁⲩ ⲡⲉ ⲡⲉⲧⲛ̄ⲉⲓⲱⲧ (16) ⲡⲉϫⲉ ⲓ̅ⲥ̅ ϫⲉ ⲧⲁⲭⲁ
32 ⲉⲩⲙⲉⲉⲩⲉ ⲛ̄ϭⲓ ⲣⲣⲱⲙⲉ ϫⲉ ⲛ̄ⲧⲁⲉⲓⲉⲓ ⲉⲛⲟⲩ
ϫⲉ ⲛ̄ⲟⲩⲉⲓⲣⲏⲛⲏ ⲉϫⲙ̄ ⲡⲕⲟⲥⲙⲟⲥ ⲁⲩⲱ
34 ⲥⲉⲥⲟⲟⲩⲛ ⲁⲛ ϫⲉ ⲛ̄ⲧⲁⲉⲓⲉⲓ ⲁⲛⲟⲩϫⲉ ⲛ̄ϩⲛ̄
ⲡⲱⲣϫ̄ ⲉϫⲛ̄ ⲡⲕⲁϩ ⲟⲩⲕⲱϩⲧ ⲟⲩⲥⲏϥⲉ
36 ⲟⲩⲡⲟⲗⲉⲙⲟⲥ ⲟⲩⲛ̄ ϯⲟⲩ ⲅⲁⲣ ⲛⲁϣⲱⲡ[ⲉ]
84 ϩⲛ̄ ⲟⲩⲏⲉⲓ ⲟⲩⲛ̄ ϣⲟⲙⲧ ⲛⲁϣⲱⲡⲉ ⲉϫⲛ̄
2 ⲥⲛⲁⲩ ⲁⲩⲱ ⲥⲛⲁⲩ ⲉϫⲛ̄ ϣⲟⲙⲧ ⲡⲉⲓⲱⲧ
ⲉϫⲙ̄ ⲡϣⲏⲣⲉ ⲁⲩⲱ ⲡϣⲏⲣⲉ ⲉϫⲙ̄ ⲡⲉⲓⲱⲧ

14 ⲛ̄ⲥⲣⲱⲡⲕ̄ sic; l. ⲛ̄ϭⲣⲱϩⲉ

10

14 the stones and burn you up.

(14) Jesus said to them: If you fast (νηστεύειν), you will

16 beget sin for yourselves, and if you

pray, you will be condemned (κατακρίνειν), and

18 if you give alms (ἐλεημοσύνη), you will do

evil (κακόν) to your spirits (πνεῦμα). And if you

20 go into any land and

wander in the regions (χώρα), if they receive (παραδέχεσθαι)

22 you, eat what they set before you,

heal (θεραπεύειν) the sick among them.

24 For (γάρ) what goes into your mouth

will not defile you, but (ἀλλά) what

26 comes out of your mouth, that is what

will defile you. (15) Jesus said: When (ὅταν)

28 you see Him who was not born

of woman, prostrate yourselves upon

30 your face and adore Him: He

is your Father. (16) Jesus said:

32 Men possibly (τάχα) think that I have come to throw

peace (εἰρήνη) upon the world (κόσμος) and

34 they do not know that I have come to throw

divisions upon the earth, fire, sword,

36 war (πόλεμος). For (γάρ) there shall be five

84　in a house: three shall be against

2 two and two against three, the father

against the son and the son against the father,

4 ⲁⲩⲱ ⲥⲉⲛⲁⲱϩⲉ ⲉⲣⲁⲧⲟⲩ ⲉⲩⲟ ⲙ̄ⲙⲟⲛⲁ

ⲭⲟⲥ (17) ⲡⲉϫⲉ ⲓ̄ⲥ̄ ϫⲉ ϯⲛⲁϯ ⲛⲏⲧⲛ̄ ⲙ̄ⲡⲉⲧⲉ

6 ⲙ̄ⲡⲉⲃⲁⲗ ⲛⲁⲩ ⲉⲣⲟϥ ⲁⲩⲱ ⲡⲉⲧⲉ ⲙ̄ⲡⲉⲙⲁ

ⲁϫⲉ ⲥⲟⲧⲙⲉϥ· ⲁⲩⲱ ⲡⲉⲧⲉ ⲙ̄ⲡⲉϭⲓϫ ϭⲙ̄

8 ϭⲱⲙϥ· ⲁⲩⲱ ⲙ̄ⲡⲉϥⲉⲓ ⲉϩⲣⲁⲓ̈ ϩⲓ ⲫⲏⲧ·

ⲣ̄ⲣⲱⲙⲉ (18) ⲡⲉϫⲉ ⲙ̄ⲙⲁⲑⲏⲧⲏⲥ ⲛ̄ⲓ̄ⲥ̄ ϫⲉ ϫⲟ

10 ⲟⲥ ⲉⲣⲟⲛ ϫⲉ ⲧⲏϩⲁⲛ ⲉⲥⲛⲁϣⲱⲡⲉ ⲛ̄

ⲁϣ ⲛ̄ϩⲉ ⲡⲉϫⲉ ⲓ̄ⲥ̄ ⲁⲧⲉⲧⲛ̄ϭⲱⲗⲡ̄· ⲅⲁⲣ ⲉⲃⲟⲗ

12 ⲛ̄ⲧⲁⲣⲭⲏ ϫⲉⲕⲁⲁⲥ ⲉⲧⲉⲧⲛⲁϣⲓⲛⲉ ⲛ̄ⲥⲁ

ⲑⲁϩⲏ ϫⲉ ϩⲙ̄ ⲡⲙⲁ ⲉⲧⲉ ⲧⲁⲣⲭⲏ ⲙ̄ⲙⲁⲩ ⲉ

14 ⲑⲁϩⲏ ⲛⲁϣⲱⲡⲉ ⲙ̄ⲙⲁⲩ ⲟⲩⲙⲁⲕⲁⲣⲓⲟⲥ

ⲡⲉⲧⲛⲁⲱϩⲉ ⲉⲣⲁⲧϥ̄ ϩⲛ̄ ⲧⲁⲣⲭⲏ ⲁⲩⲱ

16 ϥⲛⲁⲥⲟⲩⲱⲛ ⲑⲁⲏ ⲁⲩⲱ ϥⲛⲁϫⲓ ϯⲡⲉ

ⲁⲛ ⲙ̄ⲙⲟⲩ (19) ⲡⲉϫⲉ ⲓ̄ⲥ̄ ϫⲉ ⲟⲩⲙⲁⲕⲁⲣⲓⲟⲥ

18 ⲡⲉ ⲛ̄ⲧⲁϩⲣ̄ϣⲱⲡⲉ ϩⲁⲧⲉϩⲏ ⲉⲙⲡⲁⲧⲉϥϣⲱ

ⲡⲉ ⲉⲧⲉⲧⲛ̄ϣⲁⲛϣⲱⲡⲉ ⲛⲁⲉⲓ ⲙ̄ⲙⲁⲑⲏ

20 ⲧⲏⲥ ⲛ̄ⲧⲉⲧⲛ̄ⲥⲱⲧⲙ̄ ⲁⲛⲁϣⲁϫⲉ ⲛⲉⲉⲓⲱ

ⲛⲉ ⲛⲁⲣⲇⲓⲁⲕⲟⲛⲉⲓ ⲛⲏⲧⲛ̄ ⲟⲩⲛ̄ⲧⲏⲧⲛ̄

22 ⲅⲁⲣ ⲙ̄ⲙⲁⲩ ⲛ̄ⲧⲟⲩ ⲛ̄ϣⲏⲛ ϩⲙ̄ ⲡⲁⲣⲁ·

ⲇⲓⲥⲟⲥ ⲉⲥⲉⲕⲓⲙ ⲁⲛ ⲛ̄ϣⲱⲙ· ⲙ̄ⲡⲣⲱ

13 and 14 ⲑⲁϩⲏ, 16 ⲑⲁⲏ *sic*; *l.* ⲑⲁⲏ or ⲧⲁϩⲏ

15 after ⲡⲉⲧⲛⲁ there is ϩ deleted by a horizontal stroke. It looks like Achmi-
mic ϩ . But as this is not found in our text it cannot be ϩ = S ϣ 'to
be able'

22 ⲡⲁⲣⲁ *sic*; *l.* ⲡⲡⲁⲣⲁ

23 ⲉⲥⲉⲕⲓⲙ for classical Sahidic ⲉⲛⲥⲉⲕⲓⲙ

4 and they will stand as solitaries (μοναχός).

(17) Jesus said: I will give you what

6 eye has not seen and what ear

has not heard and what hand has not touched

8 and (what) has not arisen in the heart

of man. (18) The disciples (μαθητής) said to Jesus: Tell

10 us how our end will be.

Jesus said: Have you then (γάρ) discovered

12 the beginning (ἀρχή) so that you inquire about

the end? For where the beginning (ἀρχή) is,

14 there shall be the end. Blessed (μακάριος) is

he who shall stand at the beginning (ἀρχή), and

16 he shall know the end and he shall not taste

death. (19) Jesus said: Blessed (μακάριος) is

18 he who was before he came into being.

If you become disciples (μαθητής) to Me

20 and hear My words, these stones

will minister (διακονεῖν) to you.

22 For (γάρ) you have five trees in Paradise (παράδεισος),

which are unmoved in summer (or) in winter

24 ⲁⲩⲱ ⲙⲁⲣⲉⲛⲟⲩⲱⲃⲉ ⲅⲉ ⲉⲃⲟⲗ ⲡⲉⲧ·

ⲛⲁⲥⲟⲩⲱⲛⲟⲩ ϥⲛⲁϫⲓ ϯⲡⲉ ⲁⲛ· ⲙⲙⲟⲩ

26 (20) ⲡⲉϫⲉ ⲙⲙⲁⲑⲏⲧⲏⲥ ⲛⲓⲥ ϫⲉ ϫⲟⲟⲥ

ⲉⲣⲟⲛ ϫⲉ ⲧⲙⲛⲧⲉⲣⲟ ⲛⲙⲡⲏⲩⲉ ⲉⲥ

28 ⲧⲏⲧⲱⲛ ⲉⲛⲓⲙ ⲡⲉϫⲁϥ ⲛⲁⲩ ϫⲉ ⲉⲥⲧⲛ

ⲧⲱⲛ ⲁⲩⲃⲗⲃⲓⲗⲉ ⲛϣⲗⲧⲁⲙ ⲥⲟⲃⲕ ⲡⲁ

30 ⲣⲁ ⲛϭⲣⲟϭ ⲧⲏⲣⲟⲩ ϩⲟⲧⲁⲛ ⲇⲉ ⲉⲥϣⲁ

ⲅⲉ ⲉϫⲙ ⲡⲕⲁϩ ⲉⲧⲟⲩⲣ ϩⲱⲃ ⲉⲣⲟϥ ϣⲁϥ

32 ⲧⲉⲩⲟ ⲉⲃⲟⲗ ⲛⲛⲟⲩⲛⲟϭ ⲛⲧⲁⲣ ⲛϥϣⲱ

ⲡⲉ ⲛⲥⲕⲉⲡⲏ ⲛϩⲁⲗⲁⲧⲉ ⲛⲧⲡⲉ (21) ⲡⲉ

34 ϫⲉ ⲙⲁⲣⲓϩⲁⲙ ⲛⲓⲥ ϫⲉ ⲉⲛⲉⲕⲙⲁⲑⲏ

ⲧⲏⲥ ⲉⲓⲛⲉ ⲛⲛⲓⲙ ⲡⲉϫⲁϥ ϫⲉ ⲉⲩⲉⲓⲛⲉ

85 ⲛⲟⲛϣⲏⲣⲉ ϣⲏⲙ ⲉⲩ[ϭ]ⲉⲗⲓⲧ ⲁⲩϭⲱϣⲉ ⲉⲧⲱ

2 ⲟⲩ ⲁⲛ ⲧⲉ ϩⲟⲧⲁⲛ ⲉⲩϣⲁⲉⲓ ⲛϭⲓ ⲛϫⲟⲉⲓⲥ

ⲛⲧⲥⲱϣⲉ ⲥⲉⲛⲁϫⲟⲟⲥ ϫⲉ ⲕⲉ ⲧⲛⲥⲱϣⲉ

4 ⲉⲃⲟⲗ ⲛⲁⲛ ⲛⲧⲟⲟⲩ ⲥⲉⲕⲁⲕ ⲁϩⲏⲩ ⲙⲡⲟⲩⲙ

ⲧⲟ ⲉⲃⲟⲗ ⲉⲧⲣⲟⲩⲕⲁⲁⲥ ⲉⲃⲟⲗ ⲛⲁⲩ ⲛⲥⲉϯ ⲧⲟⲩ

6 ⲥⲱϣⲉ ⲛⲁⲩ ⲇⲓⲁ ⲧⲟⲩⲧⲟ ϯϫⲱ ⲙⲙⲟⲥ ϫⲉ ⲉϥ·

ϣⲁⲉⲓⲙⲉ ⲛϭⲓ ⲡϫⲉⲉ[.] ⲛⲛⲉⲓ ϫⲉ ϥⲛⲏⲩ ⲛϭⲓ

8 ⲡⲣⲉϥϫⲓⲟⲩⲉ ϥⲛⲁⲣⲟⲉⲓⲥ ⲉⲙⲡⲁⲧⲉϥ·ⲉⲓ ⲛϥⲧⲙ

ⲕⲁⲁϥ· ⲉϣⲟϫⲧ· ⲉϩⲟⲩⲛ ⲉⲡⲉϥⲏⲉⲓ ⲛⲧⲉ ⲧⲉϥ·

10 ⲙⲛⲧⲉⲣⲟ ⲉⲧⲣⲉϥϥⲓ ⲛⲛⲉϥ·ⲥⲕⲉⲩⲟⲥ ⲛⲧⲱⲧⲛ

---

29 ⲥⲟⲃⲕ *sic*; *l.* ⲉⲥⲥⲟⲃⲕ

33 ⲛϩⲁⲗⲁⲧⲉ *sic*; *l.* ⲛⲛϩⲁⲗⲁⲧⲉ

3 and 5 For ⲕⲱ ⲉⲃⲟⲗ ⲛⲁ″ with same expression for a piece of land as object, *cf.* Ryl 151,2; 159,18

7 ⲡϫⲉⲉ[.] *sic*; either for ⲡϫⲟⲉⲓⲥ or it is an unstressed form as in ⲃⲉ ⲛⲉⲗⲟⲟⲗⲉ 88, 13

24 and their leaves do not fall.

Whoever knows them will not taste death.

26 (20) The disciples (μαθητής) said to Jesus: Tell

us what the Kingdom of Heaven is

28 like. He said to them: It is like

a mustard-seed, smaller than (παρά)

30 all seeds. But (δέ) when (ὅταν) it

falls on the tilled earth, it

32 produces a large branch and becomes

shelter (σκέπη) for ‹the› birds of heaven.

34 (21) Mary said to Jesus: Whom are thy disciples (μαθητής)

like? He said: They are like

85   little children who have installed themselves in a field

2 which is not theirs. When (ὅταν) the owners of the field come,

they will say: "Release to us our field".

4 They take off their clothes before them

to release it (the field) to them and to give back

6 their field to them. Therefore (διὰ τοῦτο) I say:

If the lord of the house knows that the thief is coming,

8 he will stay awake before he comes and will not

let him dig through into his house of his

10 kingdom to carry away his goods (σκεῦος). You

ⲇⲉ ⲣⲟⲉⲓⲥ ϩⲁⲧⲉϩⲛ ⲙ̄ⲡⲕⲟⲥⲙⲟⲥ ⲙⲟⲧⲣ ⲙ̄

12 ⲙⲱⲧⲛ ⲉϫⲛ̄ ⲛⲉⲧⲛ̄ϯⲡⲉ ϩⲏⲛ ⲟⲧⲛⲟϭ ⲛ̄ⲁⲧ

ⲛⲁⲙⲓⲥ ϣⲓⲛⲁ ⲍⲉ ⲛⲉⲛⲗⲏⲥⲧⲏⲥ ϩⲉ ⲉϩⲟⲓⲏ ⲉⲉⲓ

14 ϣⲁⲣⲱⲧⲛ ⲉⲡⲉⲓ ⲧⲉⲭⲣⲉⲓⲁ ⲉⲧⲉⲧⲛ̄ϭⲱϣⲧ'

ⲉⲃⲟⲗ ϩⲏⲧⲥ̄ ⲥⲉⲛⲁϩⲉ ⲉⲣⲟⲥ ⲙⲁⲣⲉϥϣⲱⲡⲉ

16 ϩⲛ̄ ⲧⲉⲧⲛ̄ⲙⲏⲛⲧⲉ ⲛ̄ϭⲓ ⲟⲧⲣⲱⲙⲉ ⲛ̄ⲡⲓⲥⲧⲛ

ⲙⲱⲛ ⲛ̄ⲧⲁⲣⲉⲡⲕⲁⲣⲡⲟⲥ ⲡⲱϩ ⲁϥⲉⲓ ϩⲏⲛ ⲟⲧ

18 ϭⲉⲡⲏ ⲉⲡⲉϥⲁⲥϩ ϩⲛ̄ ⲧⲉϥϭⲓϫ ⲁϥϩⲁⲥϥ ⲡⲉ

ⲧⲉ ⲟⲩⲛ ⲙⲁⲁϫⲉ ⲙ̄ⲙⲟϥ' ⲉⲥⲱⲧⲙ ⲙⲁⲣⲉϥⲥⲱⲧⲙ̄

20 (22) ⲁⲓⲥ ⲛⲁⲧ ⲁϩⲛ̄ⲕⲟⲧⲉⲓ ⲉⲧϫⲓ ⲉⲣⲱⲧⲉ ⲡⲉϫⲁϥ ⲛ̄

ⲛⲉϥⲙⲁⲑⲏⲧⲏⲥ ⲍⲉ ⲛⲉⲉⲓⲕⲟⲧⲉⲓ ⲉⲧϫⲓ ⲉⲣⲱ

22 ⲧⲉ ⲉⲩⲧⲛ̄ⲧⲱⲛ ⲁⲛⲉⲧⲃⲏⲕ' ⲉϩⲟⲧⲛ ⲁⲧⲙⲛ̄

ⲧⲉⲣⲟ ⲡⲉϫⲁⲧ ⲛⲁϥ ⲍⲉ ⲉⲉⲓ ⲉⲛⲟ ⲛ̄ⲕⲟⲧⲉⲓ ⲧⲛ̄

24 ⲛⲁⲃⲱⲕ' ⲉϩⲟⲧⲛ ⲉⲧⲙⲛ̄ⲧⲉⲣⲟ ⲡⲉϫⲉ ⲓⲏⲥ ⲛⲁⲧ

ⲍⲉ ϩⲟⲧⲁⲛ ⲉⲧⲉⲧⲛ̄ϣⲁⲣ ⲡⲥⲛⲁⲧ ⲟⲧⲁ ⲁⲧⲱ ⲉ

26 ⲧⲉⲧⲛ̄ϣⲁⲣ ⲡⲥⲁ ⲛϩⲟⲧⲛ ⲛ̄ⲑⲉ ⲙ̄ⲡⲥⲁ ⲛⲃⲟⲗ

ⲁⲧⲱ ⲡⲥⲁ ⲛⲃⲟⲗ ⲛ̄ⲑⲉ ⲙ̄ⲡⲥⲁ ⲛϩⲟⲧⲛ ⲁⲧⲱ ⲡⲥⲁ̄

28 ⲧⲡⲉ ⲛ̄ⲑⲉ ⲙ̄ⲡⲥⲁ ⲙ̄ⲡⲓⲧⲛ ⲁⲧⲱ ϣⲓⲛⲁ ⲉⲧⲉ

ⲧⲛⲁⲉⲓⲣⲉ ⲙ̄ⲫⲟ'ⲟⲧⲧ' ⲙⲛ ⲧⲥϩⲓⲙⲉ ⲙ̄ⲡⲓⲟⲧⲁ

30 ⲟⲧⲱⲧ ϫⲉⲕⲁⲁⲥ ⲛⲉϥϩⲟⲟⲧⲧ' ⲣ̄ ϩⲟⲟⲧⲧ' ⲛ̄ⲧⲉ

ⲧⲥϩⲓⲙⲉ ⲣ̄ ⲥϩⲓⲙⲉ ϩⲟⲧⲁⲛ ⲉⲧⲉⲧⲛ̄ϣⲁⲉⲓⲣⲉ

32 ⲛ̄ϩⲛ̄ⲃⲁⲗ ⲉⲡⲙⲁ ⲛ̄ⲟⲧⲃⲁⲗ' ⲁⲧⲱ ⲟⲧϭⲓϫ'

ⲉⲡⲙⲁ ⲛ̄ⲛⲟⲧϭⲓϫ' ⲁⲧⲱ ⲟⲧⲉⲣⲏⲧⲉ ⲉⲡⲙⲁ

34 ⲛ̄ⲟⲧⲉⲣⲏⲧⲉ ⲟⲧϩⲓⲕⲱⲛ' ⲉⲡⲙⲁ ⲛ̄ⲟⲧϩⲓⲕⲱ

18 ϩⲁⲥϥ for classical Sahidic ⲟϩⲥϥ

23 ⲉⲉⲓ ⲉⲛⲟ for ⲉⲉⲓⲉ ⲉⲛⲟ (haplography)

33 and 34 ⲟⲧⲉⲣⲏⲧⲉ for ⲟⲧⲟⲧⲉⲣⲏⲧⲉ

16

then (δέ) must watch for the world (κόσμος), gird

12 up your loins with great strength (δύναμις)

lest (ἵνα) the brigands (λῃστής) find (a) way to come

14 to you, because (ἐπεί) they will find the advantage (χρεία)

which you expect. Let there be

16 among you a man of understanding (ἐπιστήμων);

when the fruit (καρπός) ripened, he came quickly

18 with his sickle in his hand, he reaped it.

Whoever has ears to hear let him hear.

20 (22) Jesus saw children who were being suckled. He said to

his disciples (μαθητής): These children who are being suckled

22 are like those who enter the Kingdom.

They said to Him: Shall we then, being children,

24 enter the Kingdom? Jesus said to them:

When (ὅταν) you make the two one, and

26 when you make the inner as the outer

and the outer as the inner and the above

28 as the below, and when (ἵνα)

you make the male and the female into a single one,

30 so that the male will not be male and

the female (not) be female, when (ὅταν) you make

32 eyes in the place of an eye, and a hand

in the place of a hand, and a foot in the place

34 of a foot, (and) an image (εἰκών) in the place of an image (εἰκών),

ⲧⲟⲧⲉ ⲧⲉⲧⲛⲁⲃⲱⲕˈ ⲉϩⲟⲩⲛ [ⲉⲧⲙⲛⲧⲉⲣⲟ]

86 (23) ⲡⲉϫⲉ ⲓⲥ ϫⲉ ϯⲛⲁⲥⲉⲧⲡ ⲧⲏⲛⲉ ⲟⲩⲁ ⲉⲃⲟⲗ

2 ϩⲛ ϣⲟ ⲁⲩⲱ ⲥⲛⲁⲩ ⲉⲃⲟⲗ ϩⲛ ⲧⲃⲁ ⲁⲩⲱ
ⲥⲉⲛⲁϣⲉ ⲉⲣⲁⲧⲟⲩ ⲉⲩⲟ ⲟⲩⲁ ⲟⲩⲱⲧˈ (24) ⲡⲉ

4 ϫⲉ ⲛⲉϥⲙⲁⲑⲏⲧⲏⲥ ϫⲉ ⲙⲁⲧⲥⲉⲃⲟⲛˈ ⲉⲡⲧⲟ
ⲡⲟⲥ ⲉⲧⲕⲙⲙⲁⲩ ⲉⲡⲉⲓ ⲧⲁⲛⲁⲅⲕⲏ ⲉⲣⲟⲛ ⲧⲉ

6 ⲉⲧⲣⲛϣⲓⲛⲉ ⲛⲥⲱϥˈ ⲡⲉϫⲁϥˈ ⲛⲁⲩ ϫⲉ ⲡⲉⲧⲉⲩ
ⲛ ⲙⲁⲁϫⲉ ⲙⲙⲟϥ ⲙⲁⲣⲉϥˈⲥⲱⲧⲙ ⲟⲩⲛ ⲟⲩ

8 ⲟⲉⲓⲛˈ ϣⲟⲟⲡ ⲙⲫⲟⲩⲛ ⲛⲛⲟⲩⲣⲙⲟⲩⲟⲉⲓⲛ
ⲁⲩⲱ ϥⲣ ⲟⲩⲟⲉⲓⲛ ⲉⲡⲕⲟⲥⲙⲟⲥ ⲧⲏⲣϥˈ ⲉϥⲧⲙ

10 ⲣ ⲟⲩⲟⲉⲓⲛˈ ⲟⲩⲕⲁⲕⲉ ⲡⲉ (25) ⲡⲉϫⲉ ⲓⲥ ϫⲉ ⲙⲉⲣⲉ
ⲡⲉⲕⲥⲟⲛ ⲛⲑⲉ ⲛⲧⲉⲕˈⲯⲩⲭⲏ ⲉⲣⲓⲧⲏⲣⲉⲓ ⲙⲙⲟϥ

12 ⲛⲑⲉ ⲛⲧⲉⲗⲟⲩ ⲙⲡⲉⲕˈⲃⲁⲗˈ (26) ⲡⲉϫⲉ ⲓⲥ ϫⲉ ⲡϫⲏ
ⲉⲧϩⲙ ⲡⲃⲁⲗ ⲙⲡⲉⲕˈⲥⲟⲛ ⲕⲛⲁⲩ ⲉⲣⲟϥˈ ⲡⲥⲟⲉⲓ

14 ϫⲉ ⲉⲧϩⲙ ⲡⲉⲕⲃⲁⲗ ⲕⲛⲁⲩ ⲁⲛ ⲉⲣⲟϥˈ ϩⲟⲧⲁⲛ
ⲉⲕϣⲁⲛⲛⲟⲩϫⲉ ⲙⲡⲥⲟⲉⲓ ⲉⲃⲟⲗ ϩⲙ ⲡⲉⲕˈ

16 ⲃⲁⲗ ⲧⲟⲧⲉ ⲕⲛⲁⲛⲁⲩ ⲉⲃⲟⲗ ⲉⲛⲟⲩϫⲉ ⲙⲡϫⲏ
ⲉⲃⲟⲗ ϩⲙ ⲡⲃⲁⲗ ⲙⲡⲉⲕⲥⲟⲛ (27) ⲉⲧⲉⲧⲙⲣⲛⲏ

18 ⲥⲧⲉⲩⲉ ⲉⲡⲕⲟⲥⲙⲟⲥ ⲧⲉⲧⲛⲁϩⲉ ⲁⲛ ⲉⲧⲙⲛⲧⲉ
ⲣⲟ ⲉⲧⲉⲧⲛⲧⲙⲉⲓⲣⲉ ⲙⲡⲥⲁⲙⲃⲁⲧⲟⲛ ⲛⲥⲁⲃˈ

20 ⲃⲁⲧⲟⲛ ⲛⲧⲉⲧⲛⲁⲛⲁⲩ ⲁⲛ ⲉⲡⲉⲓⲱⲧ' (28) ⲡⲉϫⲉ
ⲓⲥ ϫⲉ ⲁⲉⲓⲱϩⲉ ⲉⲣⲁⲧˈ ϩⲛ ⲧⲙⲏⲧⲉ ⲙⲡⲕⲟⲥ

---

17 ⲉⲧⲉⲧⲙ *sic*; l. ⲉⲧⲉⲧⲛⲧⲙ.   Before it ⲡⲉϫⲉ ⲓⲥ ϫⲉ is omitted

then (τότε) shall you enter [the Kingdom].

86   (23) Jesus said: I shall choose you, one out

2 of a thousand, and two out of ten thousand, and
they shall stand as a single one.

4 (24) His disciples (μαθητής) said: Show us the place (τόπος)
where Thou art, for (ἐπεί) it is necessary (ἀνάγκη) for us

6 to seek it. He said to them: Whoever has
ears let him hear. Within a man of light

8 there is light
and he lights the whole world (κόσμος). When he

10 does not shine, there is darkness. (25) Jesus said: Love
thy brother as thy soul (ψυχή), guard (τηρεῖν) him

12 as the apple of thine eye. (26) Jesus said: The mote
that is in thy brother's eye thou seest,

14 but (δέ) the beam that is in thine eye, thou seest not. When (ὅταν)
thou castest the beam out of thine

16 eye, then (τότε) thou wilt see clearly to cast the mote
out of thy brother's eye. (27) < Jesus said:> If you fast (νηστεύειν) not

18 from the world (κόσμος), you will not find the Kingdom;
if you keep not the Sabbath (σάββατον) as Sabbath (σάββατον),

20 you will not see the Father.

    (28) Jesus said: I took my stand in the midst of the world (κόσμος)

---

3 "single one"; same sense as μοναχός in p. 84, 4.
12 "apple"; lit.: "pupil".
19 "keep .. as Sabbath"; lit.: "make into Sabbath", translates: σαββατίζειν.

22 мос аүω лειоүωнϩ εϐολ нлү ϩ̄н сарϩ
    лειϩε εροοү тнроү εүтлϩε м̄пϩρε ελλ

24 лү м̄ϩнтоү εϥоϐε лүω лтлψүхн † тклс
    εϫη нϣнре н̄рρωμε ϫε ϩη̄ϐλλεεү

26 ε не ϩ̄м поүϩнт· лүω сенлү εϐολ лн
    ϫε н̄тлүει επκοсμος εүϣоүειт· εү·

28 ϣιне он етроүει εϐολ ϩ̄м пκοсμος
    εүϣоүειт πλнн тεноү сетоϩε ϩο

30 тлн εүϣлннεϩ поүнрп· тοτε сенлр
    метлноει (29) пεϫε ῑс εϣϫε н̄тлтсарϩ·

32 ϣωпе етϐе пνл оүϣпнре те εϣ
    ϫε пνл δε етϐе псωμл оүϣпнре

34 н̄ϣпнре пε· ллл лнок· †ρ̄ ϣпнре
87 м̄плει ϫε πω[с τε]ϵιноϭ м̄мнтрмм

2 о лсоүωϩ ϩ̄н τεειμ̄нтϩнκε (30) пεϫε ῑс
    ϫε пμл еүн̄ ϣομт н̄ноүте м̄млү ϩ̄н

4 ноүте не пμл еүн̄ снлү н оүл лнок
    †ϣооп· н̄ммлϥ· (31) пεϫε ῑс м̄н профн

6 тнс ϣнп· ϩ̄м пεϥ†ме млресоειн ροε
    рлпеүе н̄нет·сооүн м̄моϥ· (32) пεϫε ῑс

8 ϫε оүπολις εүκωт м̄мос ϩιϫ̄н оүто
    оү εϥϫосе естлϫрнτ м̄н ϭομ н̄сϩε

10 оүδε снлϣ ϩωп· лн (33) пεϫε ῑс пετ·кнл
    сωтм̄ εроϥ ϩ̄м пεκ·мллϫε ϩ̄м пκεμл

12 лϫε тлϣεοειϣ’ м̄моϥ ϩιϫ̄н нετнϫε

32 and 33 пνл *sic*; *l.* ппνл
34 пε *sic*; *l.* те

22 and in flesh (σάρξ) I appeared to them;
   I found them all drunk, I found none

24 among them athirst. And my soul (ψυχή) was afflicted
   for the sons of men, because they are blind

26 in their heart and do not see
   that empty they have come into the world (κόσμος)

28 (and that) empty they seek to go out of the world (κόσμος) again.
   But (πλήν) now they are drunk.

30 When (ὅταν) they have shaken off their wine, then (τότε) will **they**
   repent (μετανοεῖν). (29) Jesus said: If the flesh (σάρξ)

32 has come into existence because of ‹the› spirit (πνεῦμα), it is a marvel;
   but (δέ) if ‹the› spirit (πνεῦμα) (has come into existence) because of

34 it is a marvel of marvels. But (ἀλλά) I marvel   [the body (σῶμα),

87 at how (πῶς) this great wealth

2 has made its home in this poverty. (30) Jesus said:
   Where there are three gods,

4 they are gods; where there are two or (ἤ) one, I
   am with him. (31) Jesus said: No prophet (προφήτης)

6 is acceptable in his village, no physician heals (θεραπεύειν)
   those who know him. (32) Jesus said:

8 A city (πόλις) being built on a high mountain
   (and) fortified can not fall

10 nor (οὐδέ) can it (ever) be hidden. (33) Jesus said: What thou shalt
   hear in thine ear (and) in the other ear,

12 that preach from your housetops;

27 "that", or "because".

ⲙⲉⲡⲱⲣ ⲙⲁⲣⲉⲗⲁⲁⲧ˙ ⲅⲁⲣ ϫⲉⲣⲉ ϩⲏⲃⲥ ⲛϥˋ

14 ⲕⲁⲁϥ˙ ϩⲁ ⲙⲁⲁϫⲉ ⲟⲩⲇⲉ ⲙⲁϥⲕⲁⲁϥˋ ϩⲙ ⲙⲁ
ⲉϥϩⲏⲡˋ ⲁⲗⲗⲁ ⲉϣⲁⲣⲉϥⲕⲁⲁϥ ϩⲓϫⲛ ⲧⲗⲩ

16 ⲭⲛⲓⲁ ϫⲉⲕⲁⲁⲥ ⲟⲩⲟⲛ ⲛⲓⲙˋ ⲉⲧⲃⲏⲕˋ ⲉϩⲟⲩⲛ
ⲁⲩⲱ ⲉⲧⲛⲏⲩ ⲉⲃⲟⲗ ⲉⲩⲛⲁⲛⲁⲩ ⲁⲡⲉϥⲟⲩ

18 ⲟⲉⲓⲛ (34) ⲡⲉϫⲉ ⲓ̅ⲥ̅ ϫⲉ ⲟⲩⲃⲗⲗⲉ ⲉϥϣⲁⲛⲥⲱⲕ
ϩⲏⲧϥˋ ⲛ̅ⲛⲟⲩⲃⲗⲗⲉ ϣⲁⲩϩⲉ ⲙⲡⲉⲥⲛⲁⲩ

20 ⲉⲡⲉⲥⲏⲧˋ ⲉⲩϩⲓⲉⲓⲧˋ (35) ⲡⲉϫⲉ ⲓ̅ⲥ̅ ⲙⲛ ϭⲟⲙ
ⲛ̅ⲧⲉⲟⲩⲁ ⲃⲱⲕˋ ⲉϩⲟⲩⲛ ⲉⲡⲏⲓ ⲙ̅ⲡϫⲱ

22 ⲱⲣⲉ ⲛ̅ϥϫⲓⲧϥˋ ⲛ̅ϫⲛⲁϩ ⲉⲓⲙⲏⲧⲓ ⲛ̅ϥⲙⲟⲩⲣ
ⲛ̅ⲛⲉϥϭⲓϫˋ ⲧⲟⲧⲉ ϥⲛⲁⲡⲱⲱⲛⲉ ⲉⲃⲟⲗ

24 ⲙ̅ⲡⲉϥⲏⲉⲓ (36) ⲡⲉϫⲉ ⲓ̅ⲥ̅ ⲙⲛ̅ϥⲓ ⲣⲟⲟⲩϣ ϫⲓ
ϩⲧⲟⲟⲩⲉ ϣⲁ ⲣⲟⲩϩⲉ ⲁⲩⲱ ϫⲓⲛ ϩⲓⲣⲟⲩϩⲉ

26 ϣⲁ ϩⲧⲟⲟⲩⲉ ϫⲉ ⲟⲩ ⲡⲉ ⲉⲧⲛⲁⲧⲁⲁϥ ϩⲓⲱⲧˋ
ⲧⲏⲩⲧⲛ (37) ⲡⲉϫⲉ ⲛⲉϥⲙⲁⲑⲏⲧⲏⲥ ϫⲉ ⲁϣ ⲛ̅

28 ϩⲟⲟⲩ ⲉⲕⲛⲁⲟⲩⲱⲛϩ ⲉⲃⲟⲗ ⲛⲁⲛ ⲁⲩⲱ ⲁϣ
ⲛ̅ϩⲟⲟⲩ ⲉⲛⲁⲛⲁⲩ ⲉⲣⲟⲕˋ ⲡⲉϫⲉ ⲓ̅ⲥ̅ ϫⲉ ϩⲟ

30 ⲧⲁⲛ ⲉⲧⲉⲧⲛϣⲁⲕⲉⲕ ⲧⲏⲩⲧⲛ ⲉϩⲟⲩ ⲙ̅ⲡⲉ
ⲧⲛ̅ϣⲓⲡⲉ ⲁⲩⲱ ⲛ̅ⲧⲉⲧⲛϥⲓ ⲛ̅ⲛⲉⲧⲛ̅ϣⲧⲏⲛ

32 ⲛ̅ⲧⲉⲧⲛⲕⲁⲁⲩ ϩⲁ ⲡⲉⲥⲏⲧ ⲛ̅ⲛⲉⲧⲛⲟⲩⲉⲣⲏ
ⲧⲉ ⲛ̅ⲑⲉ ⲛ̅ⲛⲓⲕⲟⲩⲉⲓ ⲛ̅ϣⲏⲣⲉ ϣⲏⲙˋ ⲛ̅ⲧⲉ

34 ⲧⲏϫⲟⲡϫⲡ ⲙ̅ⲙⲟⲟⲩ ⲧⲟⲧ[ⲉ ⲧⲉⲧⲛⲁⲛⲁⲩ

88 ⲁ ⲡϣⲏⲣⲉ ⲙ̅ⲡⲉⲧⲟⲛϩ ⲁⲩⲱ ⲧⲉⲧⲛⲁⲣ

2 ϩⲟⲧⲉ ⲁⲛ (38) ⲡⲉϫⲉ ⲓ̅ⲥ̅ ϫⲉ ϩⲁϩ ⲛⲥⲟⲡ ⲁⲧⲉⲧⲛ̅
ⲣⲉⲡⲓⲑⲩⲙⲉⲓ ⲉⲥⲱⲧⲙ ⲁⲛⲉⲉⲓϣⲁϫⲉ ⲛⲁⲉⲓ

4 ⲉϯϫⲱ ⲙ̅ⲙⲟⲟⲩ ⲛⲏⲧⲛ ⲁⲩⲱ ⲙⲛ̅ⲧⲏⲧⲛ

30/31 ⲙ̅ⲡⲉⲧⲛ for ⲉⲙⲡⲉⲧⲛ (?)

for (γάρ) no one lights a lamp and

14 puts it under a bushel, nor (οὐδέ) does he put it in a

hidden place, but (ἀλλά) he sets it on the lampstand (λυχνία),

16 so that all who come in

and go out may see its light.

18 (34) Jesus said: If a blind man leads

a blind man, both of them fall

20 into a pit. (35) Jesus said: It is not possible

for one to enter the house of the strong (man)

22 and take him (or: it) by force unless (εἰ μή τι) he bind

his hands; then (τότε) will he ransack his house.

24 (36) Jesus said: Take no thought from

morning until evening and from evening

26 until morning for what you shall put on.

(37) His disciples (μαθητής) said: When

28 wilt Thou be revealed to us and when

will we see Thee? Jesus said: When (ὅταν)

30 you take off your clothing without

being ashamed, and take your clothes

32 and put them under your feet

as the little children and

34 tread on them, then (τότε) [shall you behold]

88 the Son of the Living (One) and you shall not fear.

2 (38) Jesus said: Many times have you

desired (ἐπιθυμεῖν) to hear these words

4 which I say to you, and you have

30/31 Or: "when you take off your shame".

ⲕⲉⲟⲩⲁ ⲉⲥⲟⲧⲙⲟⲩ ⲛⲧⲟⲟⲧϥ ⲟⲩⲛ ϩⲛϩⲟ

6 ⲟⲩ ⲛⲁϣⲱⲡⲉ ⲛⲧⲉⲧⲛϣⲓⲛⲉ ⲛⲥⲱⲉⲓ ⲧⲉ

ⲧⲛⲁϩⲉ ⲁⲛ· ⲉⲣⲟⲉⲓ· (39) ⲡⲉϫⲉ ⲓ̅ⲥ̅ ϫⲉ ⲙⲫⲁⲣⲓⲥⲁⲓ

8 ⲟⲥ ⲙⲛ ⲛⲅⲣⲁⲙⲙⲁⲧⲉⲩⲥ ⲁⲩϫⲓ ⲛϣⲁϣⲧ·

ⲛⲧⲅⲛⲱⲥⲓⲥ ⲁⲩϩⲟⲡⲟⲩ ⲟⲩⲧⲉ ⲙⲡⲟⲩⲃⲱⲕ

10 ⲉϩⲟⲩⲛ ⲁⲩⲱ ⲛⲉⲧⲟⲩⲱϣ ⲉⲃⲱⲕ· ⲉϩⲟⲩⲛ ⲙ

ⲡⲟⲩⲕⲁⲁⲩ ⲛⲧⲱⲧⲛ ⲇⲉ ϣⲱⲡⲉ ⲙⲫⲣⲟⲛⲓⲙⲟⲥ

12 ⲛⲑⲉ ⲛⲛϩⲟϥ· ⲁⲩⲱ ⲛⲁⲕⲉⲣⲁⲓⲟⲥ ⲛⲑⲉ ⲛⲛ

ϭⲣⲟⲙ·ⲡⲉ (40) ⲡⲉϫⲉ ⲓ̅ⲥ̅ ⲟⲩⲃⲉ ⲛⲉⲗⲟⲟⲗⲉ ⲁⲩ

14 ⲧⲟϭⲥ ⲙⲡⲥⲁ ⲛⲃⲟⲗ ⲙⲡⲉⲓⲱⲧ· ⲁⲩⲱ ⲉⲥⲧⲁ

ϫⲣⲏⲩ ⲁⲛ ⲥⲉⲛⲁⲡⲟⲣⲕⲥ ϩⲁ ⲧⲉⲥⲛⲟⲩⲛⲉ ⲛⲥ

16 ⲧⲁⲕⲟ (41) ⲡⲉϫⲉ ⲓ̅ⲥ̅ ϫⲉ ⲡⲉⲧⲉⲩⲛⲧⲁϥ ϩⲛ ⲧⲉϥ·

ϭⲓϫ ⲥⲉⲛⲁϯ ⲛⲁϥ· ⲁⲩⲱ ⲡⲉⲧⲉ ⲙⲛⲧⲁϥ ⲡⲕⲉ

18 ϣⲏⲙ ⲉⲧⲟⲩⲛⲧⲁϥ· ⲥⲉⲛⲁϥⲓⲧϥ ⲛⲧⲟⲟⲧϥ·

(42) ⲡⲉϫⲉ ⲓ̅ⲥ̅ ϫⲉ ϣⲱⲡⲉ ⲉⲧⲉⲧⲛⲣⲡⲁⲣⲁⲅⲉ

20 (43) ⲡⲉϫⲁⲩ ⲛⲁϥ· ⲛϭⲓ ⲛⲉϥ·ⲙⲁⲑⲏⲧⲏⲥ ϫⲉ ⲛⲧⲁⲕ

ⲛⲓⲙ· ⲉⲕϫⲱ ⲛⲛⲁⲓ ⲛⲁⲛ· ϩⲛ ⲛⲉⲧϫⲱ ⲙ

22 ⲙⲟⲟⲩ ⲛⲏⲧⲛ ⲛⲧⲉⲧⲛⲉⲓⲙⲉ ⲁⲛ ϫⲉ ⲁⲛⲟⲕ·

ⲛⲓⲙ ⲁⲗⲗⲁ ⲛⲧⲱⲧⲛ ⲁⲧⲉⲧⲛϣⲱⲡⲉ ⲛⲑⲉ ⲛ

24 ⲛⲓⲓ̈ⲟⲩⲇⲁⲓⲟⲥ ϫⲉ ⲥⲉⲙⲉ ⲙⲡϣⲏⲛ ⲥⲉⲙⲟⲥ

ⲧⲉ ⲙⲡⲉϥⲕⲁⲣⲡⲟⲥ ⲁⲩⲱ ⲥⲉⲙⲉ ⲙⲡⲕⲁⲣⲡⲟⲥ

26 ⲥⲉⲙⲟⲥⲧⲉ ⲙⲡϣⲏⲛ (44) ⲡⲉϫⲉ ⲓ̅ⲥ̅ ϫⲉ ⲡⲉⲧⲁϫⲉ

ⲟⲩⲁ ⲁⲡⲉⲓⲱⲧ· ⲥⲉⲛⲁⲕⲱ ⲉⲃⲟⲗ ⲛⲁϥ· ⲁⲩⲱ

28 ⲡⲉⲧⲁϫⲉ ⲟⲩⲁ ⲉⲡϣⲏⲣⲉ ⲥⲉⲛⲁⲕⲱ ⲉⲃⲟⲗ

ⲛⲁϥ· ⲡⲉⲧⲁϫⲉ ⲟⲩⲁ ⲇⲉ ⲁⲡⲡ̅ⲛ̅ⲁ̅ ⲉⲧⲟⲩⲁⲃ

21 ⲡⲉϫⲉ ⲓ̅ⲥ̅ ⲛⲁⲩ ϫⲉ is omitted before ϩⲛ

24

no other from whom to hear them. There will be days

6 when you will seek Me (and)

you will not find Me. (39) Jesus said: The Pharisees (Φαρισαῖος)

8 and the Scribes (γραμματεύς) have received the keys

of Knowledge (γνῶσις), they have hidden them. They did not (οὔτε)

10 and they did not let those (enter) who wished.   [enter,

But (δέ) you, become wise (φρόνιμος)

12 as serpents and innocent (ἀκέραιος) as

doves. (40) Jesus said: A vine has been

14 planted without the Father and, as it is not

established, it will be pulled up by its roots and be

16 destroyed. (41) Jesus said: Whoever has in his

hand, to him shall be given; and whoever does not have,

18 from him shall be taken even the little which he has.

(42) Jesus said: Become passers-by (παράγειν).

20 (43) His disciples (μαθητής) said to Him:

Who art Thou that Thou should say these things to us. ‹ Jesus said to

them›: From what I say

22 to you, you do not know who I am,

but (ἀλλά) you have become as

24 the Jews ('Ιουδαῖος), for they love the tree, they hate

its fruit (καρπός) and they love the fruit (καρπός),

26 they hate the tree. (44) Jesus said: Whoever

blasphemes against the Father, it shall be forgiven him, and

28 whoever blasphemes against the Son, it shall be forgiven him;

but (δέ) whoever blasphemes against the Holy Ghost (πνεῦμα),

30 ⲥⲉⲛⲁⲕⲱ ⲁⲛ ⲉⲃⲟⲗ ⲛⲁϥ· ⲟⲩⲧⲉ ϩⲙ̄ ⲡⲕⲁϩ
ⲟⲩⲧⲉ ϩⲛ̄ ⲧⲡⲉ (45) ⲡⲉϫⲉ ⲓ̄ⲥ̄ ⲙⲁⲩϫⲉⲗⲉ ⲉⲗⲟⲟ

32 ⲗⲉ ⲉⲃⲟⲗ ϩⲛ̄ ϣⲟⲛⲧⲉ ⲟⲩⲧⲉ ⲙⲁⲩⲕⲱⲧϥ·
ⲕⲛ̄ⲧⲉ ⲉⲃⲟⲗ ϩⲛ̄ ⲥⲣϭⲁⲙⲟⲩⲗ· ⲙⲁⲩϯ ⲕⲁⲣⲡⲟⲥ

34 ⲅ[ⲁⲣ ⲟⲩⲁⲅ]ⲁⲑⲟⲥ ⲣⲣⲱⲙⲉ ϣⲁϥⲉⲓⲛⲉ ⲛ̄
89 ⲟⲩⲁⲅⲁⲑⲟⲛ ⲉⲃⲟⲗ ϩ[ⲙ̄] ⲡⲉϥⲉϩⲟ ⲟⲩⲕⲁ[ⲕⲟⲥ]

2 ⲣⲣⲱⲙⲉ ϣⲁϥⲉⲓⲛⲉ ⲛ̄ϩⲛ̄ⲡⲟⲛⲏⲣⲟⲛ ⲉⲃⲟⲗ
ϩⲙ̄ ⲡⲉϥⲉϩⲟ ⲉⲑⲟⲟⲩ ⲉⲧϩⲛ̄ ⲡⲉϥϩⲏⲧ· ⲁⲩ

4 ⲱ ⲛϥϫⲱ ⲛ̄ϩⲛ̄ⲡⲟⲛⲏⲣⲟⲛ ⲉⲃⲟⲗ ⲅⲁⲣ ϩⲙ̄
ⲫⲟⲩⲟ ⲙ̄ⲫⲏⲧ· ϣⲁϥⲉⲓⲛⲉ ⲉⲃⲟⲗ ⲛ̄ϩⲛ̄ⲡⲟ

6 ⲛⲏⲣⲟⲛ (46) ⲡⲉϫⲉ ⲓ̄ⲥ̄ ϫⲉ ϫⲓⲛ· ⲁⲇⲁⲙ ϣⲁ ⲓ̈ⲱϩⲁ
ⲛⲛⲏⲥ ⲡⲃⲁⲡⲧⲓⲥⲧⲏⲥ ϩⲛ̄ ⲛ̄ϫⲡⲟ ⲛ̄ⲛϩⲓⲟⲙⲉ

8 ⲙ̄ⲛ̄ ⲡⲉⲧϫⲟⲥⲉ ⲁⲓ̈ⲱϩⲁⲛⲛⲏⲥ ⲡⲃⲁⲡⲧⲓ
ⲥⲧⲏⲥ ϣⲓⲛⲁ ϫⲉ ⲛⲟⲩⲱϭⲡ· ⲛϭⲓ ⲛⲉϥⲃⲁⲗ

10 ⲁⲉⲓϫⲟⲟⲥ ⲇⲉ ϫⲉ ⲡⲉⲧⲛⲁϣⲱⲡⲉ ϩⲛ̄ ⲧⲏⲩ
ⲧⲏ ⲉϥ̣ⲟ ⲛ̄ⲕⲟⲩⲉⲓ ϥⲛⲁⲥⲟⲩⲱⲛ ⲧⲙ̄ⲛ̄ⲧⲉ

12 ⲣⲟ ⲁⲩⲱ ϥⲛⲁϫⲓⲥⲉ ⲁⲓ̈ⲱϩⲁⲛⲛⲏⲥ (47) ⲡⲉϫⲉ ⲓ̄ⲥ̄
ϫⲉ ⲙ̄ⲛ̄ ϭⲟⲙ ⲛ̄ⲧⲉⲟⲩⲣⲱⲙⲉ ⲧⲉⲗⲟ ⲁϩⲧⲟ

14 ⲥⲛⲁⲩ ⲛϥϫⲱⲗⲕ· ⲙ̄ⲡⲓⲧⲉ ⲥⲛ̄ⲧⲉ ⲁⲩⲱ ⲙⲛ̄
ϭⲟⲙ· ⲛ̄ⲧⲉⲟⲩϩⲙ̄ϩⲁⲗ ϣⲙ̄ϣⲉ ϫⲟⲉⲓⲥ ⲥⲛⲁⲩ

16 ⲏ ϥⲛⲁⲣⲧⲓⲙⲁ ⲙ̄ⲡⲟⲩⲁ· ⲁⲩⲱ ⲡⲕⲉⲟⲩⲁ ϥⲛⲁ
ϩⲩⲃⲣⲓⲍⲉ ⲙ̄ⲙⲟϥ· ⲙⲁⲣⲉⲣⲱⲙⲉ ⲥⲉ ⲣ̄ⲡⲁⲥ

18 ⲁⲩⲱ ⲛ̄ⲧⲉⲩⲛⲟⲩ ⲛϥ̄ⲉⲡⲓⲑⲩⲙⲉⲓ ⲁⲥⲱ ⲛⲏⲣⲡ·
ⲃ̄ⲃ̄ⲣⲣⲉ ⲁⲩⲱ ⲙⲁⲩⲛⲟⲩϫ· ⲛⲏⲣⲡ· ⲃ̄ⲃ̄ⲣⲣⲉ ⲉⲁⲥ

20 ⲕⲟⲥ ⲛ̄ⲁⲥ ϫⲉⲕⲁⲁⲥ ⲛ̄ⲛⲟⲩⲡⲱϩ ⲁⲩⲱ ⲙⲁⲩ
ⲛⲉϫ· ⲛⲏⲣⲡ· ⲛ̄ⲁⲥ ⲉⲁⲥⲕⲟⲥ ⲃ̄ⲃ̄ⲣⲣⲉ ϣⲓⲛⲁ ϫⲉ

9 ⲛⲟⲩⲱϭⲡ *sic*; *l.* ⲛⲟⲩⲟⲩⲱϭⲡ

30 it shall not be forgiven him, either (οὔτε) on earth
or (οὔτε) in heaven. (45) Jesus said: They do not harvest grapes

32 from thorns, nor (οὔτε) do they gather
figs from thistles; [for (γάρ)] they give no fruit (καρπός)

34 [A] good [(ἀγ)]αθός) man brings forth

89   good (ἀγαθόν) out of his treasure, an evil (κα[κός)]

2 man brings forth evil things (πονηρόν) out
of his evil treasure, which is in his heart, and

4 speaks evil things (πονηρόν). For (γάρ) out of
the abundance of the heart he brings forth evil things (πονηρόν).

6 (46) Jesus said: From Adam until John
the Baptist (βαπτιστής) there is among those who are born of women

8 none higher than John the Baptist (βαπτιστής),
so that (ἵνα) his eyes will not be broken.

10 But (δέ) I have said that whoever among you
becomes as a child shall know the Kingdom,

12 and he shall become higher than John. (47) Jesus said:
It is impossible for a man to mount two horses

14 and to stretch two bows, and it is impossible
for a servant to serve two masters,

16 otherwise (ἤ) he will honour (τιμᾶν) the one
and offend (ὑβρίζειν) the other. No man drinks old wine

18 and immediately desires ἐπιθυμεῖν) to drink new wine;
and they do not put new (wine into old wineskins (ἀσκός),

20 lest they burst, and they
do not put old wine into a new wineskin (ἀσκός), lest (ἵνα)

22 ⲛⲉϥⲧⲉⲕⲁϥˈ ⲙⲁⲩⲁⲁϭ ⲧⲟⲉⲓⲥ ⲛⲁⲥ ⲁϣⲧⲏ
ⲛϣⲁⲉⲓ ⲉⲡⲉⲓ ⲟⲩⲛ ⲟⲩⲡⲱⲣ ⲛⲁϣⲱⲡⲉ

24 (48) ⲡⲉϫⲉ ⲓ̅ⲥ̅ ϫⲉ ⲉⲣϣⲁⲥⲛⲁⲩ ⲣ̅ ⲉⲓⲣⲏⲛⲏ ⲙⲛ
ⲛⲟⲩⲉⲣⲏⲩ ϩⲙ ⲡⲉⲓⲏⲉⲓ ⲟⲩⲱⲧˈ ⲥⲉⲛⲁϫⲟⲟⲥ

26 ⲙ̅ⲡⲧⲁⲩ ϫⲉ ⲡⲱⲱⲛⲉ ⲉⲃⲟⲗ ⲁⲩⲱ ϥⲛⲁⲡⲱ
ⲱⲛⲉ (49) ⲡⲉϫⲉ ⲓ̅ⲥ̅ ϫⲉ ϩⲉⲛⲙⲁⲕⲁⲣⲓⲟⲥ ⲛⲉ ⲛ

28 ⲙⲟⲛⲁⲭⲟⲥ ⲁⲩⲱ ⲉⲧⲥⲟⲧⲡˈ ϫⲉ ⲧⲉⲧⲛⲁ
ϩⲉ ⲁⲧⲙⲛ̅ⲧⲉⲣⲟ ϫⲉ ⲛ̅ⲧⲱⲧⲛ ϩⲛⲉⲃⲟⲗ

30 ⲛϩⲏⲧⲥ ⲡⲁⲗⲓⲛ ⲉⲧⲉⲧⲛⲁⲃⲱⲕˈ ⲉⲙⲁⲩ (50) ⲡⲉ
ϫⲉ ⲓ̅ⲥ̅ ϫⲉ ⲉⲩϣⲁⲛϫⲟⲟⲥ ⲛⲏⲧⲛ ϫⲉ ⲛ̅ⲧⲁ

32 ⲧⲉⲧⲛ̅ϣⲱⲡⲉ ⲉⲃⲟⲗ ⲧⲱⲛ ϫⲟⲟⲥ ⲛⲁⲩ
ϫⲉ ⲛ̅ⲧⲁⲛⲉⲓ ⲉⲃⲟⲗ ϩⲙ ⲡⲟⲩⲟⲉⲓⲛ ⲡⲙⲁ

34 ⲉⲛⲧⲁⲡⲟⲩⲟⲉⲓⲛ ϣⲱⲡⲉ ⲙ̅ⲙⲁⲩ ⲉⲃⲟⲗ
ϩⲓⲧⲟⲟⲧϥˈ ⲟⲩⲁⲁⲧϥˈ ⲁϥⲱϩ[ⲉ ⲉⲣⲁⲧϥ]

90 ⲁⲩⲱ ⲁϥⲟⲩⲱⲛ̲ϩ [ⲉⲃ]ⲟⲗ ϩⲛ ⲧⲟⲩϩⲓⲕⲱⲛ ⲉⲩ
2 ϣⲁϫⲟⲟⲥ ⲛⲏⲧⲛ ϫⲉ ⲛ̅ⲧⲱⲧⲛ ⲡⲉ ϫⲟⲟⲥ
ϫⲉ ⲁⲛⲟⲛ ⲛⲉϥϣⲏⲣⲉ ⲁⲩⲱ ⲁⲛⲟⲛ ⲛ̅ⲥⲱⲧⲡˈ

4 ⲙ̅ⲡⲉⲓⲱⲧˈ ⲉⲧⲟⲛϩ ⲉⲩϣⲁⲛϫⲛⲉ ⲧⲏⲩⲧⲛ
ϫⲉ ⲟⲩ ⲡⲉ ⲡⲙⲁⲉⲓⲛ ⲙ̅ⲡⲉⲧⲛⲉⲓⲱⲧˈ ⲉⲧϩⲛ

6 ⲧⲏⲩⲧⲛ ϫⲟⲟⲥ ⲉⲣⲟⲟⲩ ϫⲉ ⲟⲩⲕⲓⲙ ⲡⲉ ⲙⲛ
ⲟⲩⲁⲛⲁⲡⲁⲩⲥⲓⲥ (51) ⲡⲉϫⲁⲩ ⲛⲁϥˈ ⲛ̅ϭⲓ ⲛⲉϥⲙⲁ

8 ⲑⲏⲧⲏⲥ ϫⲉ ⲁϣ ⲛ̅ϩⲟⲟⲩ ⲉⲧⲁⲛⲁⲡⲁⲩⲥⲓⲥ ⲛ̅
ⲛⲉⲧⲙⲟⲟⲩⲧˈ ⲛⲁϣⲱⲡⲉ ⲁⲩⲱ ⲁϣ ⲛ̅ϩⲟⲟⲩ

10 ⲉⲡⲕⲟⲥⲙⲟⲥ ⲃ̅ⲃ̅ⲣⲣⲉ ⲛⲏⲩ ⲡⲉϫⲁϥ ⲛⲁⲩ ϫⲉ
ⲧⲏ ⲉⲧⲉⲧⲛ̅ϭⲱϣⲧˈ ⲉⲃⲟⲗ ϩⲏⲧⲥ̅ ⲁⲥⲉⲓ ⲁⲗⲗⲁ

12 ⲛ̅ⲧⲱⲧⲛ̅ ⲧⲉⲧⲛⲥⲟⲟⲩⲛ ⲁⲛ ⲙ̅ⲙⲟⲥ (52) ⲡⲉϫⲁⲩ

2 ⲡⲉ *sic*; *l.* ⲛⲓⲙ

28

22 it spoil it. They do not sew an old patch on a new garment,
because (ἐπεί) there would come a rent.

24 (48) Jesus said: If two make peace (εἰρήνη) with
each other in this one house, they shall say

26 to the mountain: "Be moved", and it shall be moved.
(49) Jesus said: Blessed (μακάριος) are the

28 solitary (μοναχός) and elect, for you shall
find the Kingdom; because you come from it,

30 (and) you shall go there again (πάλιν).
(50) Jesus said: If they say to you:

32 "From where have you originated?", say to them:
"We have come from the Light,

34 where the Light has originated through
itself. It [stood]

90 and it revealed itself in their image (εἰκών)".

2 If they say to you: "(Who) are you?", say:
"We are His sons and we are the elect

4 of the Living Father". If they ask you:
"What is the sign of your Father in

6 you?", say to them: "It is a movement and a
rest" (ἀνάπαυσις). (51) His disciples (μαθητής) said to Him:

8 When will the repose (ἀνάπαυσις) of
the dead come about and when

10 will the new world (κόσμος) come? He said to them:
What you expect has come, but (ἀλλά)

12 you know it not.

2 "(Who) are you?"; Ms.: "It is you".

29

ⲛⲁϥ ⲛϭⲓ ⲛⲉϥⲙⲁⲑⲏⲧⲏⲥ ⲍⲉ ⲍⲟⲩⲧ ⲁϥⲧⲉ

14 ⲙⲡⲣⲟⲫⲏⲧⲏⲥ ⲁⲩϣⲁⲍⲉ ϩⲙ ⲡⲓⲥⲣⲁⲏⲗ`

ⲁⲩⲱ ⲁⲩϣⲁⲍⲉ ⲧⲏⲣⲟⲩ ϩⲣⲁⲓ ⲛϩⲏⲧⲕ` ⲡⲉ

16 ⲍⲁϥ ⲛⲁⲩ ⲍⲉ ⲁⲧⲉⲧⲛⲕⲱ ⲙⲡⲉⲧⲟⲛϩ ⲙⲡⲉ

ⲧⲏⲙⲧⲟ ⲉⲃⲟⲗ ⲁⲩⲱ ⲁⲧⲉⲧⲛϣⲁⲍⲉ ϩⲁ ⲛⲉⲧ

18 ⲙⲟⲟⲩⲧ` (53) ⲡⲉⲍⲁⲩ ⲛⲁϥ ⲛϭⲓ ⲛⲉϥⲙⲁⲑⲏⲧⲏⲥ

ⲍⲉ ⲡⲥⲃⲃⲉ ⲣ̄ⲱⲫⲉⲗⲉⲓ ⲏ ⲙⲙⲟⲛ ⲡⲉⲍⲁϥ`

20 ⲛⲁⲩ ⲍⲉ ⲛⲉϥⲣⲱⲫⲉⲗⲉⲓ ⲛⲉⲡⲟⲩⲉⲓⲱⲧ` ⲛⲁ

ⲍⲡⲟⲟⲩ ⲉⲃⲟⲗ ϩⲛ ⲧⲟⲩⲙⲁⲁⲩ ⲉⲩⲥⲃⲃⲏⲩ

22 ⲁⲗⲗⲁ ⲡⲥⲃⲃⲉ ⲙⲙⲉ ϩⲙ ⲡⲛⲁ ⲁϥϭⲛ ϩⲏⲩ

ⲧⲏⲣϥ` (54) ⲡⲉⲍⲉ ⲓ̄ⲥ̄ ⲍⲉ ϩⲛⲙⲁⲕⲁⲣⲓⲟⲥ ⲛⲉ ⲛϩⲏ

24 ⲕⲉ ⲍⲉ ⲧⲱⲧⲛ ⲧⲉ ⲧⲙⲛⲧⲉⲣⲟ ⲛⲙⲡⲏⲩⲉ`

(55) ⲡⲉⲍⲉ ⲓ̄ⲥ̄ ⲍⲉ ⲡⲉⲧⲁⲙⲉⲥⲧⲉ ⲡⲉϥ`ⲉⲓⲱⲧ`

26 ⲁⲛ` ⲙⲛ ⲧⲉϥⲙⲁⲁⲩ ϥⲛⲁϣ ⲣ̄ ⲙⲁⲑⲏⲧⲏⲥ ⲁⲛ

ⲛⲁⲉⲓ ⲁⲩⲱ ⲛ̄ϥⲙⲉⲥⲧⲉ ⲛⲉϥ`ⲥⲛⲏⲩ ⲙⲛ

28 ⲛⲉϥⲥⲱⲛⲉ ⲛ̄ϥϥⲓ ⲙⲡⲉϥⲥⳁⲟⲥ ⲛⲧⲁϩⲉ

ϥⲛⲁϣⲱⲡⲉ ⲁⲛ ⲉϥⲟ ⲛⲁⳁⲓⲟⲥ ⲛⲁⲉⲓ (56) ⲡⲉ

30 ⲍⲉ ⲓ̄ⲥ̄ ⲍⲉ ⲡⲉⲧⲁϩⲥⲟⲩⲱⲛ ⲡⲕⲟⲥⲙⲟⲥ ⲁϥ`

ϩⲉ ⲉⲩⲡⲧⲱⲙⲁ ⲁⲩⲱ ⲡⲉⲛⲧⲁϩϩⲉ ⲉⲁⲡⲧⲱ

32 ⲙⲁ ⲡⲕⲟⲥⲙⲟⲥ ⲙⲡϣⲁ ⲙⲙⲟϥ ⲁⲛ (57) ⲡⲉ

ⲍⲉ ⲓ̄ⲥ̄ ⲍⲉ ⲧⲙⲛⲧⲉⲣⲟ ⲙⲡⲉⲓⲱⲧ` ⲉⲥⲧⲛ̄ⲧⲱ

34 ⲁⲩⲣⲱⲙⲉ ⲉⲩⲛⲧⲁϥ ⲙⲙⲁⲩ ⲛ̄ⲛⲟⲩϭⲣⲟϭ

[ⲉⲛⲁⲛⲟⲩ]ϥ` ⲁⲡⲉϥⲍⲁⲍⲉ ⲉⲓ ⲛ̄ⲧⲟⲩϣⲏ`

91 ⲁϥⲥⲓⲧⲉ ⲛ̄ⲟⲩⳁⲓⳁⲁⲛⲓⲟⲛ ⲙⲛ ⲡⲉϭⲣⲟ[ϭ ⲉ]

31 ⲡⲉⲛⲧⲁϩϩⲉ: the second ϩ is added above the line
31 ⲉⲁⲡⲧⲱ *sic*; *l.* ⲉⲩⲡⲧⲱ

(52) His disciples (μαθητής) said to Him: Twenty-four
14 prophets (προφήτης) spoke in Israel
and they all spoke about (lit.: in) Thee.
16 He said to them: You have dismissed the Living (One)
who is before you and you have spoken about the
18 dead. (53) His disciples (μαθητής) said to Him:
Is circumcision profitable (ὠφελεῖν) or (ἤ) not? He said
20 to them: If it were profitable (ὠφελεῖν), their father
would beget them circumcised from their mother.
22 But (ἀλλά) the true circumcision in Spirit (πνεῦμα) has
become profitable in every way. (54) Jesus said: Blessed (μακάριος)
24 for yours is the Kingdom of Heaven.   [are the poor,
(55) Jesus said: Whoever does not hate his father
26 and his mother will not be able to be a disciple (μαθητής) to Me,
and (whoever does not) hate his brethren and
28 his sisters and (does not) take up his cross (σταυρός) in My way
will not be worthy (ἄξιος) of Me.
30 (56) Jesus said: Whoever has known the world (κόσμος) has found
a corpse (πτῶμα), and whoever has found a corpse (πτῶμα),
32 of him the world (κόσμος) is not worthy.
(57) Jesus said: The Kingdom of the Father is like
34 a man who had [good] seed.
His enemy came by night,
91   he sowed a weed (ζιζάνιον) among the good seed.

31

2 тнанотɥ · ⲙ̄пепрѡⲙⲉ ⲕⲟⲟⲧ ⲉⲣѡ̄ⲗⲉ
ⲙ̄пϫιϫⲁⲛιⲟⲛ пⲉϫⲁɥ ⲛⲁⲧ ϫⲉ ⲙⲏпѡⲥ
4 ⲛ̄ⲧⲉⲧⲛ̄ⲃѡⲕ ϫⲉ ⲉⲛⲁⲣѡ̄ⲗⲉ ⲙ̄пϫιϫⲁⲛιⲟ
ⲛ̄ⲧⲉⲧⲛ̄ⲣѡ̄ⲗⲉ ⲙ̄пⲥⲟⲧⲟ ⲛ̄ⲙ̄ⲙⲁɥ · ϩⲙ̄ ⲫⲟ
6 ⲟⲧ ⲅⲁⲣ ⲙ̄пѡⲣⲥ ⲛ̄ϫιϫⲁⲛιⲟⲛ ⲛⲁⲟⲧѡⲛϩ
ⲉⲃⲟ̄ⲗ · ⲥⲉϩⲟ̄ⲗⲟⲧ ⲛ̄ⲥⲉⲣⲟⲕϩⲟⲧ (58) пⲉϫⲉ ῑⲥ̄
8 ϫⲉ ⲟⲧⲙⲁⲕⲁⲣιⲟⲥ пⲉ пⲣѡⲙⲉ ⲛ̄ⲧⲁϩϩιⲥⲉ
ⲁɥϩⲉ ⲁпѡ̄ⲛϩ (59) пⲉϫⲉ ῑⲥ̄ ϫⲉ ϭѡⲱⲧ ⲛ̄ⲥⲁ пⲉ
10 ⲧⲟⲛϩ ϩⲱⲥ ⲉⲧⲉⲧⲛ̄ⲟⲛϩ ϩιⲛⲁ ϫⲉ ⲛⲉⲧⲙ̄ⲙⲟⲧ
ⲁⲧⲱ ⲛ̄ⲧⲉⲧⲛ̄ϣιⲛⲉ ⲉⲛⲁⲧ ⲉⲣⲟɥ ⲁⲧⲱ ⲧⲉⲧⲛⲁϣ
12 ϭⲙ̄ϭⲟⲙ ⲁⲛ ⲉⲛⲁⲧ (60) ⲁⲧⲥⲁⲙⲁⲣⲉιⲧⲏⲥ ⲉɥϥⲓ ⲛ̄
ⲛⲟⲧϩιⲉιⲃ̄ · ⲉɥⲃⲏⲕ̄ · ⲉϩⲟⲧⲛ̄ ⲉⲧⲟⲧⲇⲁιⲁ пⲉ
14 ϫⲁɥ̄ · ⲛ̄ⲛⲉɥ̄ⲙⲁⲑⲏⲧⲏⲥ ϫⲉ пⲏ ⲙ̄пⲕⲱⲧⲉ
ⲙ̄пⲉϩιⲉιⲃ̄ · пⲉϫⲁⲧ ⲛⲁɥ̄ ϫⲉⲕⲁⲁⲥ ⲉɥⲛⲁ
16 ⲙⲟⲟⲧⲧɥ̄ · ⲛ̄ɥⲟⲧⲟⲙɥ̄ · пⲉϫⲁɥ ⲛⲁⲧ ϩⲱⲥ ⲉ
ɥⲟⲛϩ ɥⲛⲁⲟⲧⲟⲙɥ̄ · ⲁⲛ ⲁ̄ⲗ̄ⲗⲁ ⲉɥϣⲁⲙⲟ
18 ⲟⲧⲧɥ̄ · ⲛ̄ɥϣⲱпⲉ ⲛ̄ⲟⲧпⲧѡ̄ⲙⲁ пⲉϫⲁⲧ
ϫⲉ ⲛ̄ⲕⲉⲥⲙⲟⲧ ɥⲛⲁϣ ⲁⲥ ⲁⲛ пⲉϫⲁɥ ⲛⲁⲧ
20 ϫⲉ ⲛ̄ⲧⲱⲧⲛ̄ ϩⲱⲧ̄ ⲧⲏⲧⲛ̄ ϣⲓⲛⲉ ⲛ̄ⲥⲁ ⲟⲧ
ⲧⲟпⲟⲥ ⲛ̄ⲏⲧⲛ̄ ⲉϩⲟⲧⲛ̄ ⲉⲧⲁⲛⲁпⲁⲧⲥⲓⲥ
22 ϫⲉⲕⲁⲁⲥ ⲛ̄ⲛⲉⲧⲛ̄ϣⲱпⲉ ⲙ̄пⲧѡ̄ⲙⲁ ⲛ̄ⲥⲉ
ⲟⲧⲱ̄ⲙ̄ · ⲧⲏⲧⲛ̄ (61) пⲉϫⲉ ῑⲥ̄ ⲟⲧⲛ̄ ⲥⲛⲁⲧ ⲛⲁⲙ̄

12 At the beginning of (60) ⲁⲧⲛⲁⲧ is omitted by haplography

2 The man did not permit them (the workers) to pull up
   the weed (ζιζάνιον). He said to them: Lest perhaps (μήπως)
4 you go to pull up the weed (ζιζάνιον)
   and pull up the wheat with it.
6 For (γάρ) on the day of harvest the weeds (ζιζάνιον) will appear,
   they (will) pull them and burn them. (58) Jesus said:
8 Blessed (μακάριος) is the man who has suffered,
   he has found the Life. (59) Jesus said: Look upon the
10 Living (One) as long as (ὡς) you live, lest (ἵνα) you die
   and seek to see Him and be unable
12 to see. (60) ‹They saw› a Samaritan carrying
   a lamb on his way to Judea.
14 He said to His disciples (μαθητής): (Why does) this man (carry) the
   lamb with him?. They said to Him: In order that he may
16 kill it and eat it. He said to them: As long as (ὡς)
   it is alive, he will not eat it, but (ἀλλά) (only) if he has
18 killed it and it has become a corpse (πτῶμα). They said:
   Otherwise he will not be able to do it. He said to them:
20 You yourselves, seek a
   place (τόπος) for yourselves in Repose (ἀνάπαυσις),
22 lest you become a corpse (πτῶμα) and be eaten.
   (61) Jesus said: Two will rest

4 "to pull up"; lit.: "saying: "We will pull up".
13 "on his way": lit.: "going".
14-15 lit.: "He concerning (or: around) the lamb". The text must be corrupt.

24 ⲧⲟⲛ ⲙ̄ⲙⲁⲩ ϩⲓ ⲟⲩⲥⲗⲟϭ ⲡⲟⲩⲁ ⲛⲁⲙⲟⲩ ⲡⲟⲩ

ⲁ ⲛⲁϣⲛ̄ϩ ⲡⲉϫⲉ ⲥⲁⲗⲱⲙⲏ ⲛ̄ⲧⲁⲕ· ⲛⲓⲙ·

26 ⲡⲣⲱⲙⲉ ϩⲱⲥ ⲉⲃⲟⲗ ϩⲛ̄ ⲟⲩⲁ ⲁⲕⲧⲉⲗⲟ ⲉϫⲙ̄

ⲡⲁⲥⲗⲟϭ ⲁⲩⲱ ⲁⲕ·ⲟⲩⲱⲙ ⲉⲃⲟⲗ ϩⲛ̄ ⲧⲁ

28 ⲧⲣⲁⲡⲉⲍⲁ ⲡⲉϫⲉ ⲓ̄ⲥ̄ ⲛⲁⲥ ϫⲉ ⲁⲛⲟⲕ· ⲡⲉ

ⲡⲉⲧϣⲟⲟⲡ· ⲉⲃⲟⲗ ϩⲙ̄ ⲡⲉⲧϣⲏϣ ⲁⲩϯ

30 ⲛⲁⲉⲓ ⲉⲃⲟⲗ ϩⲛ̄ ⲛⲁ ⲡⲁⲉⲓⲱⲧ· ⲁⲛⲟⲕ· ⲧⲉⲕ·

ⲙⲁⲑⲏⲧⲏⲥ ⲉⲧⲃⲉ ⲡⲁⲉⲓ ϯϫⲱ ⲙ̄ⲙⲟⲥ ϫⲉ

32 ϩⲟⲧⲁⲛ ⲉϥϣⲁϣⲱⲡⲉ ⲉϥϣⲏϥ· ϥⲛⲁⲙⲟⲩϩ

ⲟⲩⲟⲉⲓⲛ ϩⲟⲧⲁⲛ ⲇⲉ ⲉϥϣⲁⲛϣⲱⲡⲉ ⲉϥ

34 ⲡⲏϣ ϥⲛⲁⲙⲟⲩϩ ⲛ̄ⲕⲁⲕⲉ (62) ⲡⲉϫⲉ [ⲓ̄]ⲥ̄ ϫⲉ ⲉⲓ

ϫⲱ ⲛ̄ⲛⲁⲙⲩⲥⲧⲏⲣⲓⲟⲛ ⲛ̄ⲛ[ⲉⲧⲙⲡϣⲁ ⲛ

92   ⲛⲁ]ⲙⲩⲥⲧⲏⲣⲓⲟⲛ ⲡⲉ[ⲧ]ⲉ ⲧⲉⲕⲟⲩⲛⲁⲙ ⲛⲁⲁϥ

2 ⲙ̄ⲛ̄ⲧⲣⲉⲧⲉⲕϩⲃⲟⲩⲣ· ⲉⲓⲙⲉ ϫⲉ ⲉⲥⲣ ⲟⲩ (63) ⲡⲉϫⲉ ⲓ̄ⲥ̄

ϫⲉ ⲛⲉⲩⲛ ⲟⲩⲣⲱⲙⲉ ⲙ̄ⲡⲗⲟⲩⲥⲓⲟⲥ ⲉⲩⲛ̄ⲧⲁϥ ⲙ̄

4 ⲙⲁⲩ ⲛ̄ϩⲁϩ ⲛ̄ⲭⲣⲏⲙⲁ ⲡⲉϫⲁϥ ϫⲉ ϯⲛⲁⲣ̄ⲭⲣⲱ ⲛ̄

ⲛⲁⲭⲣⲏⲙⲁ ϫⲉⲕⲁⲁⲥ ⲉⲉⲓⲛⲁϫⲟ ⲛ̄ⲧⲁⲱⲥϩ

6 ⲛ̄ⲧⲁⲧⲱϭⲉ ⲛ̄ⲧⲁⲙⲟⲩϩ ⲛ̄ⲛⲁⲉϩⲱⲣ ⲛ̄ⲕⲁⲣ

ⲡⲟⲥ ϣⲓⲛⲁ ϫⲉ ⲛ̄ⲣ ϭⲣⲱϩ ⲗ̄ⲗⲁⲁⲩ ⲛⲁⲉⲓ ⲛⲉ

8 ⲛⲉϥⲙⲉⲉⲧⲉ ⲉⲣⲟⲟⲩ ϩⲙ̄ ⲡⲉϥϩⲏⲧ· ⲁⲩⲱ ϩⲛ̄

ⲧⲟⲩϣⲏ ⲉⲧⲙ̄ⲙⲁⲩ ⲁϥⲙⲟⲩ ⲡⲉⲧⲉⲙ̄ ⲙⲁϫⲉ

10 ⲙ̄ⲙⲟϥ· ⲙⲁⲣⲉϥ·ⲥⲱⲧⲙ̄ (64) ⲡⲉϫⲉ ⲓ̄ⲥ̄ ϫⲉ ⲟⲩⲣⲱ

ⲙⲉ ⲛⲉⲩⲛ̄ⲧⲁϥ ϩⲛ̄ϣⲙ̄ⲙⲟ ⲁⲩⲱ ⲛ̄ⲧⲁⲣⲉϥⲥⲟⲃ

30 ⲡⲉϫⲉ ⲥⲁⲗⲱⲙⲏ ϫⲉ (or the like) is omitted before ⲁⲛⲟⲕ

31 ⲡⲉϫⲉ ⲓ̄ⲥ̄ ⲛⲁⲥ ϫⲉ (or the like) is omitted after ⲙⲁⲑⲏⲧⲏⲥ

32 ϣⲏϥ *sic*; *l*. ϣⲏϣ ?

35 *cf*. BG 32, 18/19

5 ⲱⲥϩ: after ⲱ there is ϩ cancelled by a horizontal stroke

24 on a bed: the one will die, the one
will live.   Salome said: Who art thou,

26 man, and (ὡς) whose (son)? Thou didst take thy place upon
my bench and eat from my

28 table (τράπεζα). Jesus said to her: I am He
who is from the Same,

30 to Me was given from the things of My Father. ‹Salome said›: I
am Thy disciple (μαθητής). ‹Jesus said to her›: Therefore I say,

32 if (ὅταν) he is the Same, he will be filled
with light, but (δέ) if (ὅταν) he is

34 divided, he will be filled with darkness. (62) Jesus said: I
tell My mysteries (μυστήριον) to those [who are worthy

92 of my] mysteries (μυστήριον).   What thy right (hand) will do,

2 let not thy left (hand) know what it does. (63) Jesus said:
There was a rich (πλούσιος) man who had

4 much money (χρῆμα). He said: I will use (χρῆσθαι)
my money (χρῆμα) that I may sow and reap

6 and plant and fill my storehouses with fruit (καρπός),
so that (ἵνα) I lack nothing. This was

8 what he thought in his heart. And
that night he died. Whoever has ears

10 let him hear. (64) Jesus said: A man
had guest-friends, and when he had prepared

26 Lit: as from whom (ὡς ἐκ τίνος;). Ms.: as from somebody (ὡς ἐκ τινός).

12 ⲧⲉ ⲙ̄ⲡⲁⲓⲡⲛⲟⲛ ⲁϥϫⲟⲟⲩ ⲙ̄ⲡⲉϥϩⲙ̄ϩⲁⲗ̄ ϣⲓ

ⲛⲁ ⲉϥⲛⲁⲧⲱϩⲙ̄ ⲛ̄ⲛϣ̄ⲙ̄ⲙⲟⲉⲓ ⲁϥⲃⲱⲕ̀ ⲙ̄

14 ⲡϣⲟⲣⲡ̀ ⲡⲉϫⲁϥ ⲛⲁϥ ϫⲉ ⲡⲁϫⲟⲉⲓⲥ ⲧⲱϩⲙ̄

ⲙ̄ⲙⲟⲕ· ⲡⲉϫⲁϥ ϫⲉ ⲟⲩⲏⲧⲁⲉⲓ ϩⲛ̄ϩⲣⲟⲙⲧ̀

16 ⲁϩⲉⲛⲉⲙⲡⲟⲣⲟⲥ ⲥⲉⲛⲏⲩ ϣⲁⲣⲟⲉⲓ ⲉⲣⲟⲩϭⲉ

ϯⲛⲁⲃⲱⲕ̀ ⲛ̄ⲧⲁⲟⲩⲉⲣⲥⲁϩⲛⲉ ⲛⲁⲩ ϯⲣ̄ⲡⲁⲣⲁⲓ

18 ⲧⲉⲓ ⲙ̄ⲡⲁⲓⲡⲛⲟⲛ ⲁϥⲃⲱⲕ̀ ϣⲁ ⲕⲉⲟⲩⲁ ⲡⲉ

ϫⲁϥ ⲛⲁϥ ϫⲉ ⲁⲡⲁϫⲟⲉⲓⲥ ⲧⲱϩⲙ̄ ⲙ̄ⲙⲟⲕ̀

20 ⲡⲉϫⲁϥ ⲛⲁϥ ϫⲉ ⲁⲉⲓⲧⲟⲟⲩ ⲟⲩⲏⲉⲓ ⲁⲩⲱ ⲥⲉ

ⲣⲁⲓⲧⲉⲓ ⲙ̄ⲙⲟⲉⲓ ⲛ̄ⲟⲩϩⲛⲙⲉⲣⲁ ϯⲛⲁⲥϭϥⲉ ⲁ̄

22 ⲁϥⲉⲓ ϣⲁ ⲕⲉⲟⲩⲁ ⲡⲉϫⲁϥ ⲛⲁϥ ϫⲉ ⲡⲁϫⲟ

ⲉⲓⲥ ⲧⲱϩⲙ̄ ⲙ̄ⲙⲟⲕ̀ ⲡⲉϫⲁϥ ⲛⲁϥ ϫⲉ ⲡⲁϣⲃⲏⲣ

24 ⲛⲁⲣ̄ ϣⲉⲗⲉⲉⲧ ⲁⲩⲱ ⲁⲛⲟⲕ̀ ⲉⲧⲛⲁⲣ̄ ⲇⲓⲡⲛⲟⲛ

ϯⲛⲁϣ ⲓ ⲁⲛ ϯⲣ̄ⲡⲁⲣⲁⲓⲧⲉⲓ ⲙ̄ⲡⲁⲓⲡⲛⲟⲛ· ⲁϥ̀

26 ⲃⲱⲕ̀ ϣⲁ ⲕⲉⲟⲩⲁ ⲡⲉϫⲁϥ ⲛⲁϥ ϫⲉ ⲡⲁϫⲟⲉⲓⲥ

ⲧⲱϩⲙ̄ ⲙ̄ⲙⲟⲕ̀ ⲡⲉϫⲁϥ ⲛⲁϥ̀ ϫⲉ ⲁⲉⲓⲧⲟⲟⲩ ⲛ̄

28 ⲟⲩⲕⲱⲙⲏ ⲉⲉⲓⲃⲏⲕ̀ ⲁϫⲓ ⲛ̄ϣⲟⲙ ϯⲛⲁϣ ⲓ

ⲁⲛ ϯⲣ̄ⲡⲁⲣⲁⲓⲧⲉⲓ ⲁϥⲉⲓ ⲛ̄ϭⲓ ⲡϩⲙ̄ϩⲁⲗ̄ ⲁϥϫⲟ

30 ⲟⲥ ⲁⲡⲉϥϫⲟⲉⲓⲥ ϫⲉ ⲛⲉⲛⲧⲁⲕ̀ⲧⲁϩⲙⲟⲩ ⲁ

ⲡⲁⲓⲡⲛⲟⲛ ⲁⲩⲡⲁⲣⲁⲓⲧⲉⲓ ⲡⲉϫⲉ ⲡϫⲟⲉⲓⲥ ⲙ̄

32 ⲡⲉϥϩⲙ̄ϩⲁⲗ̄ ϫⲉ ⲃⲱⲕ̀ ⲉⲡⲥⲁ ⲛⲃⲟⲗ ⲁⲛϩⲓⲟ

ⲟⲩⲉ ⲛⲉⲧⲕⲛⲁϩⲉ ⲉⲣⲟⲟⲩ ⲉⲛⲓⲟⲩ ϫⲉⲕⲁⲁⲥ

34 ⲉⲩⲛⲁⲣ̄ⲇⲓⲡⲛⲉⲓ ⲛ̄ⲣⲉϥⲧⲟⲟⲩ ⲙⲛ̄ ⲛⲉϣⲟ

[ⲧⲉ ⲉⲩⲛⲁⲃⲱ]ⲕ ⲁⲛ̀ ⲉϩⲟⲩⲛ̀ ⲉⲛⲧⲟⲡⲟⲥ ⲙ̄ⲡⲁⲓⲱⲧ̀

12 the dinner (δεῖπνον), he sent his servant to (ἵνα)
   invite the guest-friends. He went to
14 the first, he said to him: "My master invites
   thee". He said: "I have some claims
16 against some merchants (ἔμπορος); they will come to me in the evening;
   I will go and give them my orders. I pray to be excused (παραιτεῖσθαι)
18 from the dinner (δεῖπνον)". He went to another,
   he said to him: "My master has invited thee".
20 He said to him: "I have bought a house and they
   request (αἰτεῖν) me for a day (ἡμέρα). I will have no time".
22 He came to another, he said to him: "My master
   invites thee". He said to him: "My friend
24 is to be married and I am to arrange a dinner (δεῖπνον);
   I shall not be able to come. I pray to be excused (παραιτεῖσθαι) from the
26 He went to another, he said to him: "My master   [dinner" (δεῖπνον).
   invites thee". He said to him: "I have bought
28 a farm (κώμη), I go to collect the rent. I shall not be able to come.
   I pray to be excused" (παραιτεῖσθαι). The servant came, he said
30 to his master: "Those whom thou hast invited to
   the dinner (δεῖπνον) have excused (παραιτεῖσθαι) themselves". The
32 his servant: "Go out to the roads,   [master said to
   bring those whom thou shalt find, so that
34 they may dine (δειπνεῖν). Tradesmen and merchants
   [shall] not [enter] the places (τόπος) of my Father".

21 "me for a day", or "a day from me".

93   (65) πεχαϥ ϫε ογρωμε ⲛ̄χρη[cτ]ⲟ̄c ⲛⲉγⲛ[ταϥ]

2 ⲛ̄ογⲙⲁ ⲛ̄ⲉλⲟⲟλⲉ αϥτααϥ ⲛ̄[ϩ]ⲛ̄ογⲟⲉⲓⲉ

  ϣⲓⲛⲁ ⲉγⲛⲁⲣ̄ ϩωⲃˋ ⲉⲣⲟϥ ⲛ̄ϥϫⲓ ⲙ̄ⲡⲉϥⲕⲁⲣˋ

4 ⲡⲟⲥ ⲛ̄τⲟⲟⲧⲟγ αϥϫⲟⲟγ ⲙ̄ⲡⲉϥϩⲙ̄ϩⲁλ̄ ϫⲉ

  ⲕⲁⲁc ⲉⲛⲟγⲟⲉⲓⲉ ⲛⲁϯ ⲛⲁϥˋ ⲙ̄ⲡⲕⲁⲣⲡⲟc ⲙ̄

6 ⲡⲙⲁ ⲛ̄ⲉλⲟⲟλⲉ αγⲉⲙⲁⲣⲧⲉ ⲙ̄ⲡⲉϥϩⲙ̄ϩⲁλ̄

  αγϩⲓⲟγⲉ ⲉⲣⲟϥˋ ⲛⲉⲕⲉⲕⲟγⲉⲓ ⲡⲉ ⲛ̄cⲉⲙⲟⲟγⲧϥ̄ˋ

8 αⲡϩⲙ̄ϩⲁλ̄ ⲃⲱⲕˋ αϥϫⲟⲟc ⲉⲡⲉϥϫⲟⲉⲓc ⲡⲉ

  ϫⲉ ⲡⲉϥϫⲟⲉⲓc ϫⲉ ⲙⲉϣⲁⲕˋ ⲙ̄ⲡⲉϥˋcⲟγⲱ

10 ⲛⲟγ αϥϫⲟⲟγ ⲛ̄ⲕⲉϩⲙ̄ϩⲁλ̄ ⲁⲛⲟγⲟⲉⲓⲉ ϩⲓ

  ⲟγⲉ ⲉⲡⲕⲉⲟγⲁ τⲟτⲉ αⲡϫⲟⲉⲓc ϫⲟⲟγ ⲙ̄

12 ⲡⲉϥϣⲏⲣⲉ ⲡⲉϫⲁϥˋ ϫⲉ ⲙⲉϣⲁⲕˋ cⲉⲛⲁϣⲓⲡⲉ

  ϩⲏⲧϥˋ ⲙ̄ⲡⲁϣⲏⲣⲉ ⲁⲛˋⲟγⲟⲉⲓⲉ ⲉⲧⲙ̄ⲙⲁγ ⲉⲡⲉⲓ

14 cⲉcⲟⲟγⲛ ϫⲉ ⲛ̄τⲟϥ ⲡⲉ ⲡⲉⲕλⲏⲣⲟⲛⲟⲙⲟc

  ⲙ̄ⲡⲙⲁ ⲛ̄ⲉλⲟⲟλⲉ αγϭⲟⲡϥˋ αγⲙⲟⲟγⲧϥ̄ˋ

16 ⲡⲉⲧⲉⲩⲛ̄ ⲙⲁⲁϫⲉ ⲙ̄ⲙⲟϥˋ ⲙⲁⲣⲉϥˋcⲱⲧⲙ̄ (66) ⲡⲉ

  ϫⲉ ⲓ̄c̄ ϫⲉ ⲙⲁⲧcⲉⲃⲟⲉⲓ ⲉⲡⲱⲛⲉ ⲡⲁⲉⲓ ⲛ̄ⲧⲁγ

18 cⲧⲟϥˋ ⲉⲃⲟλˋ ⲛ̄ϭⲓ ⲛⲉⲧˋⲕⲱⲧˋ ⲛ̄ⲧⲟϥ ⲡⲉ ⲡⲱⲱ

  ⲛⲉ ⲛ̄ⲕⲱϩ (67) ⲡⲉϫⲉ ⲓ̄c̄ ϫⲉ ⲡⲉⲧcⲟⲟγⲛ ⲙ̄ⲡⲧⲏⲣϥˋ

20 ⲉϥⲣ̄ ϭⲣⲱϩ ⲟγⲁⲁϥ ⲣ̄ ϭⲣⲱϩ ⲙ̄ⲡⲙⲁ ⲧⲏⲣϥˋ

  (68) ⲡⲉϫⲉ ⲓ̄c̄ ϫⲉ ⲛ̄τⲱⲧⲛ̄ ϩⲙ̄ⲙⲁⲕⲁⲣⲓⲟc ϩⲟτⲁ

22 ⲉγϣⲁⲛⲙⲉcⲧⲉ ⲧⲏγⲧⲛ̄ ⲛ̄cⲉⲣ̄ⲇⲓⲱⲕⲉ ⲙ̄

  ⲙⲱⲧⲛ̄ αγⲱ cⲉⲛⲁϩⲉ ⲁⲛ ⲉⲧⲟⲡⲟc ϩⲙ̄ ⲡⲙⲁ

24 ⲉⲛⲧⲁγⲇⲓⲱⲕⲉ ⲙ̄ⲙⲱⲧⲛ̄ ϩⲣⲁⲓ̈ ⲛ̄ϩⲏⲧϥˋ (69) ⲡⲉ

9/10 ⲙ̄ⲡⲉϥcⲟγⲧⲱⲛⲟγ probably for ⲙ̄ⲡⲟγcⲟγⲧⲱⲛϥ

93   (65) He said: A good (χρηστός) man had

2 a vineyard. He gave it to husbandmen

so that (ἵνα) they would work it and that he would receive its fruit

4 from them. He sent his servant so that   [(καρπός)

the husbandmen would give him the fruit (καρπός) of

6 the vineyard. They seized his servant,

they beat him; a little longer and they would have killed him.

8 The servant came, he told it to his master.

His master said: "Perhaps he did not know them".

10 He sent another servant; the husbandmen beat

him as well. Then (τότε) the owner sent

12 his son. He said: "Perhaps they will respect

my son". Since (ἐπεί) those husbandmen

14 knew that he was the heir (κληρονόμος)

of the vineyard, they seized him, they killed him.

16 Whoever has ears let him hear.

(66) Jesus said: Show me the stone which

18 the builders have rejected; it is the corner-stone.

(67) Jesus said: Whoever knows the All

20 but fails (to know) himself lacks everything.

(68) Jesus said: Blessed (μακάριος) are you when (ὅταν)

22 you are hated and persecuted (διώκειν);

and no place (τόπος) will be found there

24 where you have been persecuted (διώκειν).

9 read: "perhaps they did not recognize him".
23-24 read: "you will find a place, where you will not be persecuted".

ϫⲉ ⲓ̅ⲥ̅ ϩⲙ̅ⲙⲁⲕⲁⲣⲓⲟⲥ ⲛⲉ ⲛⲁⲉⲓ ⲛ̅ⲧⲁⲧ̅ϫ̅ⲱⲕⲉ

26 ⲙ̅ⲙⲟⲟⲩ ϩⲣⲁⲓ̈ ϩⲙ̅ ⲡⲟⲩϩⲏⲧ` ⲛⲉⲧⲙ̅ⲙⲁⲩ`
ⲛⲉⲛⲧⲁϩⲥⲟⲩⲱⲛ ⲡⲉⲓⲱⲧ` ϩⲛ̅ ⲟⲩⲙⲉ ϩⲙ̅

28 ⲙⲁⲕⲁⲣⲓⲟⲥ ⲛⲉⲧϩⲕⲁⲉⲓⲧ` ϣⲓⲛⲁ ⲉⲧⲛⲁ
ⲧⲥⲓⲟ ⲛ̅ⲑⲏ ⲙ̅ⲡⲉⲧⲟⲩⲱϣ (70) ⲡⲉϫⲉ ⲓ̅ⲥ̅ ϩⲟ

30 ⲧⲁⲛ ⲉⲧⲉⲧⲛ̅ϣⲁϫⲡⲉ ⲡⲏ ϩⲛ̅ ⲧⲏⲩⲧⲛ̅ ⲡⲁⲓ̈
ⲉⲧⲉⲩⲛ̅ⲧⲏⲧⲛ̅ϥ ϥⲛⲁⲧⲟⲩϫⲉ ⲧⲏⲩⲧⲛ̅ ⲉϣⲱ

32 ⲡⲉ ⲙ̅ⲛ̅ⲧⲏⲧⲛ̅ ⲡⲏ ϩⲛ̅ [ⲧⲏⲩ]ⲧⲛ̅ ⲡⲁⲉⲓ ⲉⲧⲉ
ⲙ̅ⲛ̅ⲧⲏⲧⲛ̅ϥ ϩⲛ̅ ⲧⲏⲛⲉ ϥ[ⲛⲁⲙ]ⲟⲩⲧ` ⲧⲏⲛⲉ

34 (71) ⲡⲉϫⲉ ⲓ̅ⲥ̅ ϫⲉ ϯⲛⲁϣⲟⲣ[ϣⲣ ⲙ̅ⲡⲉⲉⲓ]ⲏⲉⲓ
ⲁⲩⲱ ⲙ̅ⲛ̅ ⲗⲁⲁⲩ ⲛⲁϣ ⲕⲟⲧϥ [ⲁⲛ ⲛ̅ⲕⲉⲥⲟ]ⲡ

94 (72) [ⲡⲉϫ]ⲉ ⲟ[ⲩⲣⲱⲙⲉ] ⲛⲁϥ ϫⲉ ϫⲟⲟⲥ ⲛ̅ⲛⲁⲥⲛⲏⲩ

2 ϣⲓⲛⲁ ⲉⲧⲛ[ⲁ]ⲡⲱϣⲉ ⲛ̅ⲛ̅ϩⲛⲁⲁⲩ ⲙ̅ⲡⲁⲉⲓⲱⲧ`
ⲛⲙ̅ⲙⲁⲉⲓ ⲡⲉϫⲁϥ ⲛⲁϥ ϫⲉ ⲱ ⲡⲣⲱⲙⲉ ⲛⲓⲙ

4 ⲡⲉ ⲛ̅ⲧⲁϩⲁⲁⲧ` ⲛ̅ⲣⲉϥⲡⲱϣⲉ ⲁϥⲕⲟⲧϥ ⲁ`
ⲛⲉϥⲙⲁⲑⲟⲛⲧⲏⲥ ⲡⲉϫⲁϥ ⲛⲁⲩ ϫⲉ ⲙⲏ ⲉⲉⲓ

6 ϣⲟⲟⲡ` ⲛ̅ⲣⲉϥ`ⲡⲱϣⲉ (73) ⲡⲉϫⲉ ⲓ̅ⲥ̅ ϫⲉ ⲡⲱϩⲥ
ⲙⲉⲛ ⲛⲁϣⲱϥ` ⲛ̅ⲉⲣⲅⲁⲧⲏⲥ ⲇⲉ ⲥⲟⲃⲕ` ⲥⲟⲡ̅ⲥ̅

8 ⲇⲉ ⲙ̅ⲡϫⲟⲉⲓⲥ ϣⲓⲛⲁ ⲉϥⲛⲁⲛⲉϫ` ⲉⲣⲅⲁⲧⲏⲥ
ⲉⲃⲟⲗ` ⲉⲡⲱϩⲥ̅ (74) ⲡⲉϫⲁϥ ϫⲉ ⲡϫⲟⲉⲓⲥ ⲟⲩⲛ̅

10 ϩⲁϩ ⲙ̅ⲡⲕⲱⲧⲉ ⲛ̅ⲧϫⲱⲧⲉ ⲙ̅ⲛ̅ ⲗⲁⲁⲩ ⲇⲉ ϩⲛ̅
ⲧϣⲱⲛⲉ· (75) ⲡⲉϫⲉ ⲓ̅ⲥ̅ ⲟⲩⲛ̅ ϩⲁϩ ⲁϩⲉⲣⲁⲧⲟⲩ

12 ϩⲓⲣⲙ̅ ⲡⲣⲟ ⲁⲗⲗⲁ ⲙ̅ⲙⲟⲛⲁⲭⲟⲥ ⲛⲉⲧⲛⲁⲃⲱⲕ`
ⲉϩⲟⲩⲛ ⲉⲡⲙⲁ ⲛ̅ϣⲉⲗⲉⲉⲧ` (76) ⲡⲉϫⲉ ⲓ̅ⲥ̅ ϫⲉ

29 ⲛ̅ⲑⲏ ⲙ̅ⲡⲉⲧⲟⲩⲱϣ should probably be ⲛ̅ϩⲏⲧⲟⲩ ⲙ̅ⲡⲉⲧⲟⲩⲟⲩⲁ-
ϣϥ

10 ⲧⲭⲱⲧⲉ *sic; l.* ⲧϭⲱⲧⲉ

11 ⲧϣⲱⲛⲉ *sic; l.* ⲧϭⲱⲧⲉ

(69a) Jesus said: Blessed (μακάριος) are those who have been persecuted

26 in their heart; these are they   [(διώκειν)

who have known the Father in truth.

28 (69b) Blessed (μακάριος) are the hungry, for (ἵνα)

the belly of him who desires will be filled. (70) Jesus said:

30 If (ὅταν) you bring forth that within yourselves,

that which you have will save you.

32 If you do not have that within yourselves,

that which you do not have within you will kill you.

34 (71) Jesus said: I shall de[stroy this] house

and no one will be able to build it [again].

94   (72) [A man said] to Him: Tell my brethren

2 to (ἵνα) divide my father's possessions

with me. He said to him: O (ὦ) man, who

4 made Me (a) divider? He turned to

His disciples (μαθητής), he said to them: I am not a divider,

6 am I (μή)? (73) Jesus said: The harvest

is indeed (μέν) great, but (δέ) the labourers (ἐργάτης) are few;

8 but (δέ) beg the Lord to (ἵνα) send labourers (ἐργάτης)

into the harvest. (74) He said: Lord, there are

10 many around the cistern, but (δέ) nobody in

the cistern. (75) Jesus said: Many are standing

12 at the door, but (ἀλλά) the solitary (μοναχός) are the ones who will

the bridal chamber. (76) Jesus said: [enter

---

29 possibly: "they will fill their belly with what they desire".

14 ⲧⲙⲛⲧⲉⲣⲟ ⲙⲡⲉⲓⲱⲧ' ⲉⲥⲧⲛⲧⲱⲛ ⲁⲩⲣⲱⲙⲉ
ⲛⲉϣⲱⲧ' ⲉⲩⲛⲧⲁϥ' ⲙⲙⲁⲩ ⲛⲟⲩϥⲟⲣⲧⲓ

16 ⲟⲛ ⲉⲁϥϭⲉ ⲁⲩⲙⲁⲣⲅⲁⲣⲓⲧⲏⲥ ⲡⲉϣⲱⲧ'
ⲉⲧⲙⲙⲁⲩ ⲟⲩⲥⲁⲃⲉ ⲡⲉ ⲁϥϯ ⲡⲉϥⲟⲣⲧⲓⲟⲛ

18 ⲉⲃⲟⲗ ⲁϥⲧⲟⲟⲩ ⲛⲁϥ' ⲙⲡⲓⲙⲁⲣⲅⲁⲣⲓⲧⲏⲥ
ⲟⲩⲱⲧ' ⲛⲧⲱⲧⲛ ϩⲱⲧ' ⲧⲏⲩⲧⲛ ϣⲓⲛⲉ ⲛ

20 ⲥⲁ ⲡⲉϥⲉϩⲟ ⲉⲙⲁϥⲱϫⲛ ⲉϥⲙⲏⲛ' ⲉⲃⲟⲗ
ⲡⲙⲁ ⲉⲙⲁⲣⲉϫⲟⲟⲗⲉⲥ ⲧϩⲛⲟ ⲉϩⲟⲩⲛ' ⲉⲙⲁⲩ

22 ⲉⲟⲩⲱⲙ' ⲟⲩⲇⲉ ⲙⲁⲣⲉϥϥⲛⲧ ⲧⲁⲕⲟ (77) ⲡⲉϫⲉ
ⲓⲥ ϫⲉ ⲁⲛⲟⲕ ⲡⲉ ⲡⲟⲩⲟⲉⲓⲛ ⲡⲁⲉⲓ ⲉⲧϩⲓ

24 ϫⲱⲟⲩ ⲧⲏⲣⲟⲩ ⲁⲛⲟⲕ' ⲡⲉ ⲡⲧⲏⲣϥ' ⲛⲧⲁ
ⲡⲧⲏⲣϥ' ⲉⲓ ⲉⲃⲟⲗ ⲛϩⲏⲧ· ⲁⲩⲱ ⲛⲧⲁⲡⲧⲏⲣϥ'

26 ⲡⲱϩ ϣⲁⲣⲟⲉⲓ ⲡⲱϩ ⲛⲛⲟⲩϣⲉ ⲁⲛⲟⲕ'
ϯⲙⲙⲁⲩ ϥⲓ ⲙⲡⲱⲛⲉ ⲉϩⲣⲁⲓ ⲁⲩⲱ ⲧⲉⲧⲛⲁ

28 ϩⲉ ⲉⲣⲟⲉⲓ ⲙⲙⲁⲩ (78) ⲡⲉϫⲉ ⲓⲥ ϫⲉ ⲉⲧⲃⲉ ⲟⲩ
ⲁⲧⲉⲧⲛⲉⲓ ⲉⲃⲟⲗ ⲉⲧⲥⲱϣⲉ ⲉⲛⲁⲩ ⲉⲩⲕⲁϣ

30 ⲉϥⲕⲓⲙ ⲉ[ⲃⲟⲗ] ϩⲓⲧⲙ ⲡⲧⲏⲩ ⲁⲩⲱ ⲉⲛⲁⲩ
ⲉⲩⲣ[ⲱⲙⲉ ⲉϩ]ⲛϣⲧⲏⲛ ⲉⲩϭⲏⲛ ϩⲓⲱⲱⲃ·

32 [ⲉⲓⲥ ⲛⲉⲧⲛ]ⲣⲣⲱⲟⲩ ⲙⲛ ⲛⲉⲧⲙⲙⲉⲅⲓ

95 ⲥⲧⲁⲛⲟⲥ ⲛⲁⲉⲓ ⲉⲛ[ϣⲧⲏ]ⲛ [ⲉⲧ]

2 ϭⲏⲛ ϩⲓⲱⲟⲩ ⲁⲩⲱ ⲥⲉ[ⲛⲁ]ϣ ⲥⲟⲩⲛ
ⲧⲙⲉ ⲁⲛ (79) ⲡⲉϫⲉ ⲟⲩⲥϩⲓⲙ[ⲉ] ⲛⲁϥ ϩⲙ

4 ⲡⲙⲏϣⲉ ϫⲉ ⲛⲉⲉⲓⲁⲧ[ⲥ ⲛ]ⲑϩⲏ ⲛ
ⲧⲁϩϥⲓ ϩⲁⲣⲟⲕ ⲁⲩⲱ ⲛⲕⲓ[ⲃ]ⲉ ⲉⲛⲧⲁϩ

---

20 ⲡⲉϥⲉϩⲟ ('his treasure'): at first ⲡⲉϥϩⲟ ('his face') to which the second
ⲉ was added. Correct is ⲡⲉϩⲟ

22 ⲙⲁⲣⲉϥϥⲛⲧ *sic; l.* ⲙⲁⲣⲉϥⲛⲧ

14 The Kingdom of the Father is like a man,
a merchant, who possessed merchandise (φορτίον)

16 (and) found a pearl (μαργαρίτης). That merchant
was prudent. He sold the merchandise (φορτίον),

18 he bought the one pearl (μαργαρίτης) for himself.
Do you also seek for

20 the treasure which fails not, which endures,
there where no moth comes near

22 to devour and (where) no (οὐδέ) worm destroys.
(77) Jesus said: I am the Light that is above

24 them all, I am the All,
the All came forth from Me and the All

26 attained to Me. Cleave a (piece of) wood, I
am there; lift up the stone and you will

28 find Me there. (78) Jesus said: Why
did you come out into the desert? To see a reed

30 shaken by the wind? And to see
a man clothed in soft garments?

32 [See, your] kings and your great ones (μεγιστᾶνος)

95   are those who are clothed in soft [garments]

2 and they [shall] not be able to know the truth.
(79) A woman from the multitude said to Him:

4 Blessed is the womb which
bore Thee and the breasts which

6 ⲥⲁϩⲛⲟⲩϣⲕ ⲡⲉϫⲁϥ ⲛⲁ[ⲥ] ϫⲉ ⲛⲉ

ⲉⲓⲁⲧⲟⲩ ⲛ̄ⲛⲉⲛⲧⲁⲩⲥⲱⲧⲙ̄ ⲁ·

8 ⲡⲗⲟⲅⲟⲥ ⲙ̄ⲡⲉⲓⲱⲧ ⲁⲩⲁⲣⲉϩ ⲉⲣⲟϥ

ϩⲛ̄ ⲟⲩⲙⲉ ⲟⲩⲛ̄ ϩⲛ̄ϩⲟⲟⲩ ⲅⲁⲣ ⲛⲁϣⲱⲡⲉ

10 ⲛ̄ⲧⲉⲧⲛ̄ϫⲟⲟⲥ ϫⲉ ⲛⲉⲉⲓⲁⲧⲥ̄ ⲛ̄ⲑⲣⲏ ⲧⲁ

ⲉⲓ ⲉⲧⲉ ⲙ̄ⲡⲥⲱ ⲁⲩⲱ ⲛ̄ⲕⲓⲃⲉ ⲛⲁⲉⲓ ⲉⲙⲡⲟⲩ

12 † ⲉⲣⲱⲧⲉ (80) ⲡⲉϫⲉ ⲓ̅ⲥ̅ ϫⲉ ⲡⲉⲛⲧⲁⲩⲥⲟⲩⲱⲛ

ⲡⲕⲟⲥⲙⲟⲥ ⲁϥϭⲉ ⲉⲡⲥⲱⲙⲁ ⲡⲉⲛⲧⲁϩϭⲉ

14 ⲇⲉ ⲉⲡⲥⲱⲙⲁ ⲡⲕⲟⲥⲙⲟⲥ ⲙ̄ⲡϣⲁ ⲙ̄ⲙⲟϥ·

ⲁⲛ· (81) ⲡⲉϫⲉ ⲓ̅ⲥ̅ ϫⲉ ⲡⲉⲛⲧⲁϩⲣ̄ ⲣⲙ̄ⲙⲁⲟ ⲙⲁ

16 ⲣⲉϥⲣ̄ ⲣⲣⲟ ⲁⲩⲱ ⲡⲉⲧⲉⲩⲛ̄ⲧⲁϥ ⲛ̄ⲟⲩⲇⲩⲛⲁ

ⲙⲓⲥ ⲙⲁⲣⲉϥⲁⲣⲛⲁ (82) ⲡⲉϫⲉ ⲓ̅ⲥ̅ ϫⲉ ⲡⲉⲧϩⲏⲛ

18 ⲉⲣⲟⲉⲓ ⲉϥϩⲏⲛ ⲉⲧⲥⲁⲧⲉ ⲁⲩⲱ ⲡⲉⲧⲟⲩⲏⲩ·

ⲙ̄ⲙⲟⲉⲓ ϥⲟⲩⲏⲩ ⲛ̄ⲧⲙⲛ̄ⲧⲉⲣⲟ (83) ⲡⲉϫⲉ ⲓ̅ⲥ̅

20 ϫⲉ ⲛ̄ϩⲓⲕⲱⲛ ⲥⲉⲟⲩⲟⲛϩ ⲉⲃⲟⲗ ⲙ̄ⲡⲣⲱ

ⲙⲉ ⲁⲩⲱ ⲡⲟⲩⲟⲉⲓⲛ ⲉⲧⲛ̄ϩⲏⲧⲟⲩ ϥϩⲏⲡ·

22 ϩⲛ̄ ⲑⲓⲕⲱⲛ ⲙ̄ⲡⲟⲩⲟⲉⲓⲛ ⲙ̄ⲡⲉⲓⲱⲧ· ϥⲛⲁ

ϭⲱⲗⲡ· ⲉⲃⲟⲗ ⲁⲩⲱ ⲧⲉϥϩⲓⲕⲱⲛ ϩⲏⲡ·

24 ⲉⲃⲟⲗ ϩⲓⲧⲛ̄ ⲡⲉϥⲟⲩⲟⲉⲓⲛ (84) ⲡⲉϫⲉ ⲓ̅ⲥ̅ ⲛ̄ϩⲟ

ⲟⲩ ⲉⲧⲉⲧⲛ̄ⲛⲁⲩ ⲉⲡⲉⲧⲛ̄ⲉⲓⲛⲉ ϣⲁⲣⲉⲧⲛ̄

26 ·ⲣⲁϣⲉ ϩⲟⲧⲁⲛ ⲇⲉ ⲉⲧⲉⲧⲛ̄ϣⲁⲛⲛⲁⲩ·

ⲁⲛⲉⲧⲛ̄ϩⲓⲕⲱⲛ· ⲛ̄ⲧⲁϩϣⲱⲡⲉ ϩⲓ ⲧⲉⲧⲛ̄ⲉ

28 ϩⲏ ⲟⲩⲧⲉ ⲙⲁⲩⲙⲟⲩ ⲟⲩⲧⲉ ⲙⲁⲩⲟⲩⲱⲛϩ

ⲉⲃⲟⲗ ⲧⲉⲧⲛⲁϥⲓ ϩⲁ ⲟⲩⲏⲣ· (85) ⲡⲉϫⲉ ⲓ̅ⲥ̅ ϫⲉ

30 ⲛ̄ⲧⲁⲁⲇⲁⲙ ϣⲱⲡⲉ ⲉⲃⲟⲗ ϩⲛ̄ⲛ ⲟⲩⲛⲟϭ

---

6 ⲥⲁϩⲛⲟⲩϣⲕ *sic*; *l.* ⲥⲁⲛⲟⲩϣⲕ

6 nourished Thee. He said to [her]:

Blessed are those who have heard

8 the word (λόγος) of the Father (and) have kept it

in truth. For (γάρ) there will be days

10 when you will say: Blessed is the womb

which has not conceived and the breasts which have not suckled.

12 (80) Jesus said: Whoever has known

the world (κόσμος) has found the body (σῶμα), and (δέ) whoever has

14 the body (σῶμα), of him the world (κόσμος) is not worthy.   [found

(81) Jesus said: Let him who has become rich

16 become king, and let him who has power (δύναμις)

renounce (ἀρνεῖσθαι) (it). (82) Jesus said: Whoever is near

18 to me is near to the fire, and whoever is far

from me is far from the Kingdom. (83) Jesus said:

20 The images (εἰκών) are manifest to man

and the Light which is within them is hidden

22 in the Image (εἰκών) of the Light of the Father.

He will manifest himself and His Image (εἰκών) is concealed

24 by His Light. (84) Jesus said:

When you see your likeness, you

26 rejoice. But (δέ) when (ὅταν) you see

your images (εἰκών) which came into existence before you,

28 (which) neither (οὔτε) die nor (οὔτε) are manifested,

how much will you bear! (85) Jesus said:

30 Adam came into existence from a great

29 Exclamation or question.

ⲛ̄ⲧⲛⲁⲙⲓⲥ ⲙⲛ̄ ⲟⲩⲛⲟϭ ⲙ̄ⲙⲛ̄ⲧⲣⲙ̄ⲙⲁ

32 ⲟ ⲁⲩⲱ ⲙ̄ⲡⲉϥϣⲱⲡⲉ ⲉ[ϥⲙ̄ⲡ]ϣⲁ ⲙ̄ⲙⲱ

ⲧⲛ ⲛⲉⲧⲁϫⲓⲟⲥ ⲅⲁⲣ ⲡⲉ [ⲛⲉϥⲛⲁϫⲓ †]ⲡ[ⲉ]

34 ⲁⲛ ⲙ̄ⲡⲙⲟⲩ (86) ⲡⲉϫⲉ ⲓ̄ⲥ̄ ϫⲉ [ⲛ̄ⲃⲁϣⲟⲣ ⲟⲩ

96 ⲛ̄ⲧⲁ]ⲩ ⲛ̄[ⲉⲩⲃⲏⲃ] ⲁⲩⲱ ⲛ̄ϩⲁⲗⲁⲧⲉ ⲟⲩⲛ̄ⲧⲁⲩ

2 ⲙ̄ⲙⲁⲩ ⲙ̄[ⲡⲉ]ⲩⲙⲁϩ ⲡϣⲏⲣⲉ ⲇⲉ ⲙ̄ⲡⲣⲱⲙⲉ

ⲙ̄ⲛ̄ⲧⲁϥ̇ ⲛ̄ⲛ[ⲟⲩ]ⲙⲁ ⲉⲣⲓⲕⲉ̇ ⲛ̄ⲧⲉϥ̇ⲁⲡⲉ ⲛϥ̇

4 ⲙ̄ⲧⲟⲛ ⲙ̄[ⲙⲟ]ϥ (87) ⲡⲉϫⲁϥ ⲛ̄ϭⲓ ⲓ̄ⲥ̄ ϫⲉ ⲟⲩⲧⲁⲗⲁⲓ

ⲡⲱⲣⲟⲛ ⲡ[ⲉ] ⲡⲥⲱⲙⲁ ⲉⲧⲁϣⲉ ⲛ̄ⲟⲩⲥⲱⲙⲁ̇

6 ⲁⲩⲱ ⲟⲩⲧ[ⲁ]ⲗⲁⲓⲡⲱⲣⲟⲥ ⲧⲉ ⲧ̄ⲯⲩⲭⲏ ⲉⲧⲁϣⲉ

ⲛ̄ⲛⲁⲉⲓ ⲙ̄ⲡⲥⲛⲁⲩ (88) ⲡⲉϫⲉ ⲓ̄ⲥ̄ ϫⲉ ⲛⲁⲅⲅⲉⲗⲟⲥ

8 ⲛⲏⲩ ϣⲁⲣⲱⲧⲛ̄ ⲙⲛ̄ ⲛ̄ⲡⲣⲟⲫⲏⲧⲏⲥ ⲁⲩⲱ ⲥⲉ

ⲛⲁ† ⲛⲏⲧⲛ̄ ⲛ̄ⲛⲉⲧⲉⲩⲛ̄ⲧⲏⲧⲛ̄ⲥⲉ ⲁⲩⲱ̇

10 ⲛ̄ⲧⲱⲧⲛ̄ ϩⲱⲧ ⲧⲏⲩⲧⲛ̄ ⲛⲉⲧⲛ̄ⲧⲟⲧ̇ ⲧⲏⲛⲉ

ⲧⲁⲁⲩ ⲛⲁⲩ ⲛ̄ⲧⲉⲧⲛ̄ϫⲟⲟⲥ ⲛⲏⲧⲛ̄ ϫⲉ ⲁϣ ⲛ̄

12 ϩⲟⲟⲩ ⲡⲉⲧⲟⲩⲛ̄ⲛⲏⲩ ⲛ̄ⲥⲉϫⲓ ⲡⲉⲧⲉ ⲡⲱⲟⲩ

(89) ⲡⲉϫⲉ ⲓ̄ⲥ̄ ϫⲉ ⲉⲧⲃⲉ ⲟⲩ ⲧⲉⲧⲛ̄ⲉⲓⲱ ⲙ̄ⲡⲥⲁ ⲛ

14 ⲃⲟⲗ̇ ⲙ̄ⲡⲡⲟⲧⲏⲣⲓⲟⲛ ⲧⲉⲧⲛ̄ⲣ̄ⲛⲟⲉⲓ ⲁⲛ ϫⲉ

ⲡⲉⲛⲧⲁϩⲧⲁⲙⲓⲟ ⲙ̄ⲡⲥⲁ ⲛ̄ϩⲟⲩⲛ ⲛ̄ⲧⲟϥ ⲟⲛ

16 ⲡⲉⲛⲧⲁϥⲧⲁⲙⲓⲟ ⲙ̄ⲡⲥⲁ ⲛ̄ⲃⲟⲗ̇ (90) ⲡⲉϫⲉ ⲓ̄ⲏ̄ⲥ̄

ϫⲉ ⲁⲙⲏⲉⲓⲧⲛ̄ ϣⲁⲣⲟⲉⲓ̇ ϫⲉ ⲟⲩⲭⲣⲏⲥⲧⲟⲥ

18 ⲡⲉ ⲡⲁⲛⲁϩⲃ̇ ⲁⲩⲱ ⲧⲁⲙⲛ̄ⲧϫⲟⲉⲓⲥ ⲟⲩⲣ̄ⲙ̄

ⲣⲁϣ ⲧⲉ ⲁⲩⲱ ⲧⲉⲧⲛ̄ⲁϩⲉ ⲁⲩⲁⲛⲁⲩⲡⲁⲥⲓⲥ ⲛⲏ

20 ⲧⲛ̄ (91) ⲡⲉϫⲁⲩ ⲛⲁϥ̇ ϫⲉ ϫⲟⲟⲥ ⲉⲣⲟⲛ ϫⲉ

ⲛ̄ⲧⲕ ⲛⲓⲙ ϣⲓⲛⲁ ⲉⲛⲁⲣ̄ⲡⲓⲥⲧⲉⲩⲉ ⲉⲣⲟⲕ̇ ⲡⲉ

power (δύναμις) and a great wealth,

32 and (yet) he did not become worthy of you.

For (γάρ) if he had been worthy (ἄξιος), [he would] not [have tasted]

34 death. (86) Jesus said: [The foxes]

96 [have] the[ir holes] and the birds have

2 [their] nest, but (δέ) the Son of Man

has no place to lay his head and

4 to rest. (87) Jesus said: Wretched (ταλαίπωρον)

is the body (σῶμα) which depends upon a body (σῶμα),

6 and wretched (ταλαίπωρος) is the soul (ψυχή) which depends

upon these two. (88) Jesus said: The angels (ἄγγελος)

8 and the prophets (προφήτης) will come to you and they

will give you what is yours. And

10 you, too, give to them what is in your hands,

and say to yourselves: "On which

12 day will they come and receive what is theirs?"

(89) Jesus said: Why do you wash the outside

14 of the cup (ποτήριον)? Do you not understand (νοεῖν) that

he who made the inside is also he

16 who made the outside? (90) Jesus said:

Come to Me, for easy (χρηστός)

18 is My yoke and My lordship is gentle,

and you shall find repose (ἀνάπαυσις) for yourselves.

20 (91) They said to Him: Tell us

who Thou art so that (ἵνα) we may believe (πιστεύειν) in Thee.

---

7 "The angels", or "The messengers".

22 ϫⲁϥ ⲛⲁⲩ ϫⲉ ⲧⲉⲧⲛ̄ⲣⲡⲓⲣⲁⲍⲉ ⲙ̄ⲡⲣⲟ ⲛ̄ⲧⲡⲉ

ⲙ̄ⲛ ⲡⲕⲁϩ ⲁⲩⲱ ⲡⲉⲧⲛ̄ⲡⲉⲧⲛ̄ⲙ̄ⲧⲟ ⲉⲃⲟⲗ

24 ⲙ̄ⲡⲉⲧⲛ̄ⲥⲟⲩⲱⲛϥ̄’ ⲁⲩⲱ ⲡⲉⲉⲓⲕⲁⲓⲣⲟⲥ ⲧⲉ

ⲧⲛ̄ⲥⲟⲟⲩⲛ ⲁⲛ ⲛ̄ⲣⲡⲓⲣⲁⲍⲉ ⲙ̄ⲙⲟϥ’ (92) ⲡⲉϫⲉ

26 ⲓ̄ⲥ̄ ϫⲉ ϣⲓⲛⲉ ⲁⲩⲱ ⲧⲉⲧⲛⲁϭⲓⲛⲉ ⲁⲗⲗⲁ ⲛⲉ

ⲧⲁⲧⲉⲧⲛ̄ϫⲛⲟⲩⲉⲓ ⲉⲣⲟⲟⲩ ⲛ̄ⲛⲓϩⲟⲟⲩ ⲉⲙ̄ⲡⲓ

28 ϫⲟⲟⲩ ⲛⲏⲧⲛ̄ ⲙ̄ⲫⲟⲟⲩ ⲉⲧⲙ̄ⲙⲁⲩ ⲧⲉⲛⲟⲩ

ⲉϩⲛⲁⲓ̈ ⲉϫⲟⲟⲩ ⲁⲩⲱ ⲧⲉⲧⲛ̄ϣⲓⲛⲉ ⲁⲛ ⲛ̄ⲥⲱ

30 ⲟⲩ (93) ⲙ̄ⲡⲣ̄ϯ ⲡⲉⲧⲟⲩⲁⲁⲃ ⲛ̄ⲛⲟⲩϩⲟⲟⲣ ϫⲉⲕⲁⲥ

ⲛⲟⲩⲛⲟϫⲟⲩ ⲉⲧⲕⲟⲡⲣⲓⲁ ⲙ̄ⲡⲣ̄ⲛⲟⲩϫⲉ ⲛ̄ⲙ̄

32 ⲙⲁⲣⲅⲁⲣⲓⲧ[ⲏⲥ ⲛ̄]ⲛⲉϣⲁⲧ ϣⲓⲛⲁ ϫⲉ ⲛⲟⲩⲁⲁϥ’

* * ⲁⲁ[± 4 (94) ⲡⲉϫⲉ] ⲓ̄ⲥ̄ ⲡⲉⲧϣⲓⲛⲉ ϥⲛⲁϭⲓⲛⲉ

34 [ⲁⲩⲱ ⲡⲉⲧⲧⲱϩⲙ ⲉ]ϩⲟⲩⲛ ⲥⲉⲛⲁⲟⲩⲱⲛ ⲛⲁϥ’

(95) [ⲡⲉϫⲁϥ ⲛϭⲓ ⲓ̄ⲥ̄] ⲉϣⲱⲡⲉ ⲟⲩⲛ̄ⲧⲏⲧⲛ̄ ϩⲟⲙ̄ⲧ’

After this page two pages of the MS. have been left empty.

97 ⲙ̄ⲡⲣ̄ϯ ⲉⲧⲙ̄ⲛⲥⲉ ⲁⲗⲗⲁ ✝ [± 4] ⲙ̄ⲡⲉ[ⲧⲉ]

2 ⲧⲛⲁϫⲓⲧⲟⲩ ⲁⲛ ⲛ̄ⲧⲟⲟⲧϥ̄ (96) [ⲡⲉϫⲉ] ⲓ̄ⲥ̄ ϫⲉ ⲧⲙ̄ⲛ

ⲧⲉⲣⲟ ⲙ̄ⲡⲉⲓⲱⲧ ⲉⲥⲧⲛ̄ⲧⲱ[ⲛ ⲉⲟⲩ]ⲥϩⲓⲙⲉ

4 ⲁⲥϫⲓ ⲛ̄ⲟⲩⲕⲟⲩⲉⲓ ⲛ̄ⲥⲁⲉⲓⲣ[(ⲉ) ⲁⲥϩⲟ]ⲡϥ̄ ϩⲛ̄

ⲟⲩϣⲱⲧⲉ ⲁⲥⲁⲁϥ ⲛ̄ϩⲛ̄ⲛⲟ[ϭ] ⲛ̄ⲟⲉⲓⲕ’

6 ⲡⲉⲧⲉⲩⲛ̄ ⲙⲁⲁϫⲉ ⲙ̄ⲙⲟϥ ⲙⲁ[ⲣⲉϥ]ⲥⲱⲧⲙ·

(97) ⲡⲉϫⲉ ⲓ̄ⲥ̄ ϫⲉ ⲧⲙ̄ⲛⲧⲉⲣⲟ ⲙ̄ⲡ[ⲉⲓⲱⲧ ⲉⲥ]ⲧⲛ̄

8 ⲧⲱⲛ ⲁⲩⲥϩⲓⲙⲉ ⲉⲥϥⲓ ϩⲁ ⲟⲩϭ[ⲗⲙⲉⲉⲓ] ⲉϥ’

ⲙⲉϩ ⲛ̄ⲛⲟⲉⲓⲧ’ ⲉⲥⲙⲟⲟϣⲉ [ϩⲛ ⲟⲩ]ϩⲓⲏ·

10 ⲉⲥⲟⲩⲏⲟⲩ ⲁⲡⲙⲁⲁϫⲉ ⲙ̄ⲡϭⲗⲙ[ⲉⲉⲓ] ⲟⲩ

ⲱϭⲡ’ ⲁⲡⲛⲟⲉⲓⲧ’ ϣⲟⲩⲟ ⲛ̄ⲥⲱⲥ [ϩ]ⲓ ⲧⲉϩⲓ

12 ⲏ ⲛⲉⲥⲥⲟⲟⲩⲛ ⲁⲛ ⲡⲉ ⲛⲉⲙ̄ⲡⲉⲥⲉⲓⲙⲉ

22 He said to them: You test (πειράζειν) the face of the sky
and of the earth, and him who is before your face

24 you have not known, and
you do not know to test (πειράζειν) this moment (καιρός).

26 (92) Jesus said: Seek and you will find, but (ἀλλά) those things
which you asked me in those days, I did not

28 tell you then; now
I desire to tell them, but you do not inquire after them.

30 (93) <Jesus said:> Give not what is holy to the dogs, lest
they cast it on the dung-heap (κοπρία). Throw not the

32 pearls (μαργαρίτης) to the swine, lest (ἵνα) they make it
[   ]. (94) Jesus [said]: Whoever seeks will find

34 [and whoever knocks], it will be opened to him.
(95) [Jesus said]: If you have money,

97   do not lend at interest, but (ἀλλά) give [them] to him

2 from whom you will not receive them (back). (96) Jesus [said]:
The Kingdom of the Father is like [a] woman, (who)

4 has taken a little leaven [(and) has hidden] it in
dough (and) has made large loaves of it.

6 Whoever has ears let him hear.
(97) Jesus said: The Kingdom of the [Father] is like

8 a woman who was carrying a jar
full of meal. While she was walking [on a] distant road,

10 the handle of the jar broke.
The meal streamed out behind her on the road.

12 She did not know (it), she had noticed no

ε̣ρ̣ιϲε ⲛⲧⲁⲣⲉⲥⲡⲱϩ ⲉⲣⲟⲧⲛ ⲉⲡⲉⲥⲛⲉⲓ

14 ⲁⲥⲕⲁ ⲡϭⲗⲙⲉⲉⲓ ⲁⲡⲉⲥⲏⲧ ⲁⲥϩⲉ ⲉⲣⲟϥ ⲉϥ`
ϣⲟⲩⲉⲓⲧ` (98) ⲡⲉϫⲉ ⲓ̅ⲥ̅ ⲧⲙⲛⲧⲉⲣⲟ ⲙ̅ⲡⲉⲓⲱⲧ`

16 ⲉⲥⲧⲛⲧⲱⲛ ⲉⲩⲣⲱⲙⲉ ⲉϥⲟⲩⲱϣ ⲉⲙⲟⲩⲧ
ⲟⲩⲣⲱⲙⲉ ⲙ̅ⲙⲉⲅⲓⲥⲧⲁⲛⲟⲥ ⲁϥϣⲱⲗⲙ` ⲛ̅

18 ⲧⲥⲏϥⲉ ϩ̅ⲙ̅ ⲡⲉϥⲏⲉⲓ ⲁϥϫⲟⲧⲥ ⲛ̅ⲧϫⲟ ϫⲉ
ⲕⲁⲁⲥ ⲉϥⲛⲁⲉⲓⲙⲉ ϫⲉ ⲧⲉϥϭⲓϫ` ⲛⲁⲧⲱⲕ`

20 ⲉⲣⲟⲧⲛ ⲧⲟⲧⲉ ⲁϥϩⲱⲧⲃ̅ ⲙ̅ⲡⲙⲉⲅⲓⲥⲧⲁⲛⲟⲥ
(99) ⲡⲉϫⲉ ⲙ̅ⲙⲁⲑⲏⲧⲏⲥ ⲛⲁϥ ϫⲉ ⲛⲉⲕⲥⲛⲏⲩ

22 ⲙⲛ ⲧⲉⲕⲙⲁⲁⲩ ⲥⲉⲁϩⲉⲣⲁⲧⲟⲩ ϩⲓ ⲡⲥⲁ ⲛ
ⲃⲟⲗ ⲡⲉϫⲁϥ ⲛⲁⲩ ϫⲉ ⲛⲉⲧⲛⲛⲉⲉⲓⲙⲁ

24 ⲉⲧⲣⲉ ⲙ̅ⲡⲟⲩⲱϣ ⲙ̅ⲡⲁⲉⲓⲱⲧ` ⲛⲁⲉⲓ ⲛⲉ ̅
ⲛⲁⲥⲛⲏⲩ ⲙⲛ ⲧⲁⲙⲁⲁⲩ ⲛ̅ⲧⲟⲟⲩ ⲡⲉ ⲉⲧⲛⲁ

26 ⲃⲱⲕ` ⲉϩⲟⲩⲛ ⲉⲧⲙⲛⲧⲉⲣⲟ ⲙ̅ⲡⲁⲉⲓⲱⲧ·
(100) ⲁⲩⲧⲥⲉⲃⲉ ⲓ̅ⲥ̅ ⲁⲩⲛⲟⲩⲃ ⲁⲩⲱ ⲡⲉϫⲁⲩ ⲛⲁϥ`

28 ϫⲉ ⲛⲉⲧⲏⲡ` ⲁⲕⲁⲓⲥⲁⲣ` ⲥⲉϣⲓⲧⲉ ⲙ̅ⲙⲟⲛ ⲛ̅
ⲛ̅ϣⲱⲙ` ⲡⲉϫⲁϥ ⲛⲁⲩ ϫⲉ ϯ ⲛⲁ ⲕⲁⲓⲥⲁⲣ`

30 ⲛ̅ⲕⲁⲓⲥⲁⲣ ϯ ⲛⲁ ⲡⲛⲟⲩⲧⲉ ⲙ̅ⲡⲛⲟⲩⲧⲉ
ⲁⲩⲱ ⲡⲉⲧⲉ ⲡⲱⲉⲓ ⲡⲉ ⲙⲁⲧⲛ ⲛⲁⲉⲓϥ

32 (101) ⲡⲉⲧⲁⲙⲉⲥⲧⲉ ⲡⲉϥⲉⲓ[ⲱⲧ ⲁ]ⲛ ⲙⲛ ⲧⲉϥ`
ⲙⲁⲁⲩ ⲛ̅ⲧⲁϩⲉ ϥⲛⲁϣ ⲣ̅ ⲙ̅[ⲁⲑⲏⲧⲏ]ⲥ ⲛⲁⲉⲓ ⲁ̅

34 ⲁⲩⲱ ⲡⲉⲧⲁⲙⲣ̅ⲣⲉ ⲡⲉ[ϥⲉⲓⲱⲧ ⲁⲛ ⲙ]ⲛ̅ ⲧⲉϥ
ⲙⲁⲁⲩ ⲛ̅ⲧⲁϩⲉ ϥⲛⲁϣ ⲣ̅ ⲙ̅[ⲁⲑⲏⲧⲏⲥ ⲛⲁ]

36 ⲉⲓ ⲁⲛ ⲧⲁⲙⲁⲁⲩ ⲅⲁⲣ ⲛ̅ⲧⲁ[

98 ⲉⲃ]ⲟⲗ [ⲧⲁⲙⲁⲁⲩ] ϫⲉ ⲙ̅ⲙⲉ ⲁⲥϯ ⲛⲁⲉⲓ ⲙ̅ⲡⲱⲛϩ

2 (102) ⲡⲉϫⲉ ⲓ̅ⲥ̅ [ϫⲉ ⲟ]ⲩⲟⲉⲓ ⲛⲁⲩ ⲙ̅ⲫⲁⲣⲓⲥⲁⲓⲟⲥ ϫⲉ

33 ⲛ̅ⲧⲁϩⲉ: ⲉ added above the line

accident. After she came into her house,

14 she put the jar down, she found it empty.

(98) Jesus said: The Kingdom of the Father

16 is like a man who wishes to kill

a powerful (μεγιστᾶνος) man. He drew

18 the sword in his house, he stuck it into the wall,

in order to know whether his hand would carry through;

20 then (τότε) he slew the powerful (μεγιστᾶνος) (man).

(99) The disciples (μαθητής) said to Him: Thy brethren

22 and Thy mother are standing outside.

He said to them: Those here

24 who do the will of My Father, they are

My brethren and My mother; these are they who shall

26 enter the Kingdom of My Father.

(100) They showed Jesus a gold (coin) and said to Him:

28 Caesar's men ask taxes from us.

He said to them: Give the things of Caesar

30 to Caesar, give the things of God to God

and give Me what is Mine.

32 (101) ‹Jesus said:› Whoever does not hate his father and his

mother in My way will not be able to be a [disciple (μαθητής)] to me.

34 And whoever does [not] love [his father] and his

mother in My way will not be able to be a [disciple (μαθητής)]

36 to me, for (γάρ) My mother [   ]

98   but (δέ) [My] true [Mother] gave me the Life.

2 (102) Jesus said: Woe to them, the Pharisees (Φαρισαῖος), for

98 ⲉⲧⲉⲓⲛⲉ [ⲛ]ⲟⲩⲟⲩϩⲟⲣ· ⲉϥⲛ̄ⲕⲟⲧⲕ· ϩⲓⲭⲛ̄ ⲡⲟⲩ

4 ⲟⲛⲉϥ· ⲛ̄[ϩⲉⲛ]ⲉϩⲟⲟⲩ ⲭⲉ ⲟⲩⲧⲉ ϥⲟⲩⲱⲙ ⲁⲛ

ⲟⲩⲧⲉ ϥⲕ[ⲱ ⲁ]ⲛ ⲛ̄ⲛⲉϩⲟⲟⲩ ⲉⲟⲩⲱⲙ (103) ⲡⲉⲭⲉ ⲓ̄ⲥ̄

6 ⲭⲉ ⲟⲩⲙ[ⲁⲕⲁ]ⲣⲓⲟⲥ ⲡⲉ ⲡⲣⲱⲙⲉ ⲡⲁⲉⲓ ⲉⲧⲥⲟⲟⲩⲛ̄

ⲭⲉ ϩ[ⲛ̄ ⲁϣ] ⲙ̄ⲙⲉⲣⲟⲥ ⲉⲛ̄ⲗⲏⲥⲧⲏⲥ ⲛⲏⲩ ⲉϩⲟⲩ

8 ϣⲓⲛ[ⲁ ⲉϥⲛ̄]ⲁⲧⲱⲟⲩⲛ· ⲛ̄ϥⲥⲱⲟⲩϩ ⲛ̄ⲧⲉϥ·

ⲙⲛ̄ⲧ*[.] ⲁⲩⲱ ⲛ̄ϥⲙⲟⲩⲣ ⲙ̄ⲙⲟϥ ⲉⲭⲛ̄ ⲧⲉϥ·

10 ϯⲡⲉ [ϩⲁ] ⲧⲉϩⲏ ⲉⲙⲡⲁⲧⲟⲩⲉⲓ ⲉϩⲟⲩⲛ (104) ⲡⲉ

ⲭⲁⲩ [ⲛⲁϥ] ⲭⲉ ⲁⲙⲟⲩ ⲛ̄ⲧⲛ̄ϣⲗⲏⲗ· ⲙ̄ⲡⲟⲟⲩ

12 ⲁⲩⲱ ⲛ̄ⲧⲛ̄ⲣⲛⲏⲥⲧⲉⲩⲉ ⲡⲉⲭⲉ ⲓ̄ⲥ̄ ⲭⲉ ⲟⲩ ⲅⲁⲣ·

ⲡⲉ ⲡⲛⲟⲃⲉ ⲛ̄ⲧⲁⲉⲓⲁⲁϥ· ⲏ ⲛ̄ⲧⲁⲩϭⲣⲟ ⲉⲣⲟⲉⲓ

14 ϩⲛ̄ ⲟⲩ ⲁⲗⲗⲁ ϩⲟⲧⲁⲛ ⲉⲣϣⲁⲛⲡⲛⲩⲙⲫⲓⲟⲥ ⲉⲓ

ⲉⲃⲟⲗ ϩⲙ̄ ⲡⲛⲩⲙⲫⲱⲛ ⲧⲟⲧⲉ ⲙⲁⲣⲟⲩⲛⲏⲥ

16 ⲥⲧⲉⲩⲉ ⲁⲩⲱ ⲙⲁⲣⲟⲩϣⲗⲏⲗ· (105) ⲡⲉⲭⲉ ⲓ̄ⲥ̄ ⲭⲉ ⲡⲉ

ⲧⲛⲁⲥⲟⲩⲱⲛ ⲡⲉⲓⲱⲧ ⲙⲛ̄ ⲧⲙⲁⲁⲩ ⲥⲉⲛⲁⲙⲟⲩ

18 ⲧⲉ ⲉⲣⲟϥ· ⲭⲉ ⲡϣⲏⲣⲉ ⲙ̄ⲡⲟⲣⲛⲏ (106) ⲡⲉⲭⲉ ⲓ̄ⲥ̄ ⲭⲉ

ϩⲟⲧⲁⲛ ⲉⲧⲉⲧⲛ̄ϣⲁⲣ ⲡⲥⲛⲁⲩ ⲟⲩⲁ ⲧⲉⲧⲛⲁϣⲱ

20 ⲡⲉ ⲛ̄ϣⲏⲣⲉ ⲙ̄ⲡⲣⲱⲙⲉ ⲁⲩⲱ ⲉⲧⲉⲧⲛ̄ϣⲁⲛ

ⲭⲟⲟⲥ ⲭⲉ ⲡⲧⲟⲟⲩ ⲡⲱⲱⲛⲉ ⲉⲃⲟⲗ· ϥⲛⲁ

22 ⲡⲱⲱⲛⲉ (107) ⲡⲉⲭⲉ ⲓ̄ⲥ̄ ⲭⲉ ⲧⲙⲛ̄ⲧⲉⲣⲟ ⲉⲥⲧⲛ̄ⲧⲱ

ⲉⲩⲣⲱⲙⲉ ⲛ̄ϣⲱⲥ ⲉⲩⲛ̄ⲧⲁϥ· ⲙ̄ⲙⲁⲩ ⲛ̄ϣⲉ ⲛ̄

24 ⲉⲥⲟⲟⲩ ⲁⲟⲩⲁ ⲛ̄ϩⲏⲧⲟⲩ ⲥⲱⲣⲙ̄· ⲉⲡⲛⲟϭ ⲡⲉ

ⲁϥⲕⲱ ⲙ̄ⲡⲥⲧⲉⲯⲓⲧ ⲁϥϣⲓⲛⲉ ⲛ̄ⲥⲁ ⲡⲓⲟⲩⲁ·

26 ϣⲁⲛⲧⲉϥϩⲉ ⲉⲣⲟϥ· ⲛ̄ⲧⲁⲣⲉϥϩⲓⲥⲉ ⲡⲉⲭⲁϥ·

8 ⲥⲱⲟⲩϩ: after ⲱ there is ϩ cancelled by a horizontal stroke

they are like a dog sleeping in the

4 manger of oxen, for neither (οὔτε) does he eat

nor (οὔτε) does he allow the oxen to eat. (103) Jesus said:

6 Blessed (μακάριος) is the man who knows

i[n which] part (μέρος) (of the night) the robbers (λῃστής) will come in,

8 so that (ἵνα) he will rise and collect his

[   ] and gird up his loins

10 before they come in.

(104) They said [to Him]: Come and let us pray today

12 and let us fast (νηστεύειν). Jesus said: Which then (γάρ)

is the sin that I have committed, or (ἤ) in what have I been vanquished?

14 But (ἀλλά) when (ὅταν) the bridegroom (νύμφιος) comes

out of the bridal chamber (νυμφών), then (τότε) let them

16 fast (νηστεύειν) and let them pray. (105) Jesus said:

Whoever knows father and mother shall be called

18 the son of a harlot (πόρνη). (106) Jesus said:

When (ὅταν) you make the two one, you shall become

20 sons of Man, and when you

say: "Mountain, be moved", it will

22 be moved. (107) Jesus said: The Kingdom is like

a shepherd who had a hundred

24 sheep. One of them went astray, which was the largest.

He left behind ninety-nine, he sought for the one

26 until he found it. Having tired himself out, he said

ⲙ̄ⲡⲉⲥⲟⲟⲩ ⲍⲉ ϯⲟⲩⲟϣⲕ· ⲡⲁⲣⲁ ⲡⲥⲧⲉⲯⲓⲧ'

28 (108) ⲡⲉⲍⲉ ⲓ̄ⲥ̄ ⲍⲉ ⲡⲉⲧⲁⲥⲱ ⲉⲃⲟⲗ ϧⲛ̄ ⲧⲁⲧⲁⲡⲣⲟ

ϥⲛⲁϣⲱⲡⲉ ⲛ̄ⲧⲁϩⲉ ⲁⲛⲟⲕ ϩⲱ ϯⲛⲁϣⲱⲡⲉ

30 ⲉⲛⲧⲟϥ ⲡⲉ ⲁⲩⲱ ⲛⲉⲑⲏⲡ· ⲛⲁⲟⲩⲱⲛϩ ⲉⲣⲟϥ'

(109) ⲡⲉⲍⲉ ⲓ̄ⲥ̄ ⲍⲉ ⲧⲙ̄ⲛⲧⲉⲣⲟ ⲉⲥⲧⲛ̄ⲧⲱⲛ ⲉⲩⲣⲱ

32 ⲙⲉ ⲉⲩⲛ̄ⲧⲁϥ [ⲙ̄ⲙ]ⲁⲩ ϧⲛ̄ ⲧⲉϥⲥⲱϣⲉ ⲛ̄ⲛⲟⲩ

ⲉϩⲟ ⲉϥϩ[ⲏⲡ ⲉϥ]ⲟ ⲛ̄ⲁⲧⲥⲟⲟⲩⲛ' ⲉⲣⲟϥ ⲁⲩ

34 ⲱ ⲙ̄[ⲛ̄ⲛⲥⲁ ⲧ]ⲣⲉϥⲙⲟⲩ ⲁϥⲕⲁⲁϥ ⲙ̄ⲡⲉϥ'

[ϣⲏⲣⲉ ⲛⲉⲡ]ϣⲏⲣⲉ ⲥⲟⲟⲩⲛ ⲁⲛ ⲁϥϥⲓ'

99 ⲧⲥⲱϣⲉ ⲉⲧⲙ̄ⲙⲁⲩ ⲁϥⲧⲁⲁ[ϥ ⲉⲃⲟⲗ] ⲁⲩⲱ ⲡⲉⲛ

2 ⲧⲁϩⲧⲟⲟⲧⲥ ⲁϥⲉⲓ ⲉϥⲥⲕⲁⲓ [ⲁϥϩⲉ] ⲁⲡⲉϩⲟ ⲁϥ

ⲁⲣⲭⲉⲓ ⲛ̄ϯ ϩⲟⲙⲧ' ⲉⲧⲙ̄ⲛⲥⲉ ⲛ[ⲛⲉⲧ]ϥⲟⲩⲁϣⲟⲩ

4 (110) ⲡⲉⲍⲉ ⲓ̄ⲥ̄ ⲍⲉ ⲡⲉⲛⲧⲁϩϭⲓⲛⲉ [ⲙ̄ⲡ]ⲕⲟⲥⲙⲟⲥ

ⲛϥ̄ⲣ ⲣⲙ̄ⲙⲁⲟ ⲙⲁⲣⲉϥⲁⲣⲛⲁ ⲙ̄ⲡⲕⲟⲥⲙⲟⲥ

6 (111) ⲡⲉⲍⲉ ⲓ̄ⲥ̄ ⲍⲉ ⲙ̄ⲡⲏⲩⲉ ⲛⲁϭⲱⲗ ⲁⲩⲱ ⲡⲕⲁϩ

ⲙ̄ⲡⲉⲧⲛ̄ⲙ̄ⲧⲟ ⲉⲃⲟⲗ' ⲁⲩⲱ ⲡⲉⲧⲟⲛϩ ⲉⲃⲟⲗ ϧⲛ̄

8 ⲡⲉⲧⲟⲛϩ ϥⲛⲁⲛⲁⲩ ⲁⲛ ⲉⲙⲟⲩ ⲟⲩⲁ ϩⲟⲧⲓ ⲉⲓⲥ

ⲍⲱ ⲙ̄ⲙⲟⲥ ⲍⲉ ⲡⲉⲧⲁϩⲉ ⲉⲣⲟϥ' ⲟⲩⲁⲁϥ ⲡⲕⲟⲥ

10 ⲙⲟⲥ ⲙ̄ⲡϣⲁ ⲙ̄ⲙⲟϥ' ⲁⲛ (112) ⲡⲉⲍⲉ ⲓ̄ⲥ̄ ⲍⲉ ⲟⲩⲟⲉⲓ

ⲛ̄ⲧⲥⲁⲣ̄ϩ' ⲧⲁⲉⲓ ⲉⲧⲟϣⲉ ⲛ̄ⲧⲯⲩⲭⲏ ⲟⲩⲟⲉⲓ

12 ⲛ̄ⲧⲯⲩⲭⲏ ⲧⲁⲉⲓ ⲉⲧⲟϣⲉ ⲛ̄ⲧⲥⲁⲣ̄ϩ (113) ⲡⲉⲍⲁⲩ

ⲛⲁϥ ⲛ̄ϭⲓ ⲛⲉϥⲙⲁⲑⲏⲧⲏⲥ ⲍⲉ ⲧⲙ̄ⲛⲧⲉⲣⲟ

14 ⲉⲥⲛ̄ⲛⲏⲩ ⲛⲁϣ ⲛ̄ϩⲟⲟⲩ ⲉⲥⲛ̄ⲛⲏⲩ ⲁⲛ ϧⲛ̄ ⲟⲩ

---

27 ⲉⲥⲟⲟⲩ: ⲉⲥⲟⲩⲟ has been corrected by cancelling ⲩ and adding ⲩ after
the second ⲟ above the line

32 ϧⲛ̄: ϧ added above the line

6 ⲁⲩⲱ *sic*; *l.* ⲙ̄ⲛ

8 ⲟⲩⲁ ϩⲟⲧⲓ *sic*; *l.* ⲟⲩⲁⲉ ⲉϩⲟⲧⲉ ϩⲟⲧⲓ (haplography)

to the sheep: I love thee more than (παρά) ninety-nine.

28 (108) Jesus said: Whoever drinks from My mouth
shall become as I am and I myself will become

30 he, and the hidden things shall be revealed to him.
(109) Jesus said: The Kingdom is like a man

32 who had a
treasure [hidden] in his field, without knowing it.

34 And [after] he died, he left it to his
[son. The] son did not know (about it), he accepted

99 that field, he sold [it]. And he who bought it,

2 he went, while he was plowing [he found] the treasure.
He began (ἄρχεσθαι) to lend money to whomever he wished.

4 (110) Jesus said: Whoever has found the world (κόσμος)
and become rich, let him deny (ἀρνεῖσθαι) the world (κόσμος).

6 (111) Jesus said: The heavens will be rolled up and the earth
in your presence, and he who lives on

8 the Living (One) shall see neither death nor (οὐδέ) <fear>, because (ὅτι)
Jesus says: Whoever finds himself,

10 of him the world (κόσμος) is not worthy. (112) Jesus said: Woe
to the flesh (σάρξ) which depends upon the soul (ψυχή); woe

12 to the soul (ψυχή) which depends upon the flesh (σάρξ).
(113) His disciples (μαθητής) said to Him:

14 When will the Kingdom come? < Jesus said:> It will not come by

6 Ms. literally: "and the earth is in your presence".

99 ϭⲱϣⲧ' ⲉⲃⲟⲗ' ⲉⲧⲛⲁϫⲟⲟⲥ ⲁⲛ ϫⲉ ⲉⲓⲥ ϩⲏⲏ

16 ⲧⲉ ⲙ̄ⲡⲓⲥⲁ ⲏ ⲉⲓⲥ ϩⲏⲏⲧⲉ ⲧⲏ ⲁⲗⲗⲁ ⲧⲙ̄ⲛⲧⲉⲣⲟ
ⲙ̄ⲡⲉⲓⲱⲧ' ⲉⲥⲡⲟⲣϣ' ⲉⲃⲟⲗ ϩⲓϫⲙ̄ ⲡⲕⲁϩ ⲁⲩⲱ

18 ⲣⲣⲱⲙⲉ ⲛⲁⲩ ⲁⲛ ⲉⲣⲟⲥ (114) ⲡⲉϫⲉ ⲥⲓⲙⲱⲛ ⲡⲉⲧⲣⲟⲥ
ⲛⲁⲩ ϫⲉ ⲙⲁⲣⲉⲙⲁⲣⲓϩⲁⲙ ⲉⲓ ⲉⲃⲟⲗ ⲛ̄ϩⲏⲧⲛ̄

20 ϫⲉ ⲛⲉϩⲓⲟⲙⲉ ⲙ̄ⲡϣⲁ ⲁⲛ' ⲙ̄ⲡⲱⲛϩ ⲡⲉϫⲉ ⲓ̅ⲥ̅
ϫⲉ ⲉⲓⲥ ϩⲏⲏⲧⲉ ⲁⲛⲟⲕ' ϯⲛⲁⲥⲱⲕ' ⲙ̄ⲙⲟⲥ ϫⲉ

22 ⲕⲁⲁⲥ ⲉⲉⲓⲛⲁⲁⲥ ⲛ̄ϩⲟⲟⲩⲧ' ϣⲓⲛⲁ ⲉⲥⲛⲁϣⲱ
ⲡⲉ ϩⲱⲱⲥ ⲛ̄ⲟⲩⲡ̄ⲛⲁ ⲉϥ̄ⲟⲛϩ ⲉϥⲉⲓⲛⲉ ⲙ̄

24 ⲙⲱⲧⲛ̄ ⲛ̄ϩⲟⲟⲩⲧ ϫⲉ ⲥϩⲓⲙⲉ ⲛⲓⲙ' ⲉⲥⲛⲁⲁⲥ'
ⲛ̄ϩⲟⲟⲩⲧ' ⲥⲛⲁⲃⲱⲕ' ⲉϩⲟⲩⲛ ⲉⲧⲙ̄ⲛⲧⲉⲣⲟ

26 ⲛ̄ⲙ̄ⲡⲏⲩⲉ ⟨ ⟨ ⟨ ⟨ ⟨ ⟨ ⟨ ⟨ ⟨ ⟨ ⟨ ⟨ ⟨

ⲡⲉⲩⲁⲅⲅⲉⲗⲓⲟⲛ

28 ⲡⲕⲁⲧⲁ ⲑⲱⲙⲁⲥ

expectation; they will not say: "See,

16 here", or (ἤ): "See, there". But (ἀλλά) the Kingdom
of the Father is spread upon the earth and

18 men do not see it. (114) Simon Peter said
to them: Let Mary go out from among us,

20 because women are not worthy of the Life. Jesus said:
See, I shall lead her,

22 so that I will make her male, that (ἵνα)
she too may become a living spirit (πνεῦμα), resembling

24 you males. For every woman who makes herself
male will enter the Kingdom

26 of Heaven.

The Gospel (εὐαγγέλιον)

28   according to (κατά) Thomas

SCRIPTURAL PARALLELS AND ECHOES

Log. 1, pl. 80, 12-14: cf. *Jn.* viii, 51 and 52.

Log. 2, pl. 80, 14-16: cf., in one sense, *Mt.* vii, 7-8 = *Lk.* xi, 9-10.

Log. 3, pl. 80, 19-24: cf., in one sense, *Deut.* xxx, 11-14 and *Rom.* x, 6-8; pl. 80, 25: *Lk.* xvii, 21*b*.

Log. 4, pl. 81, 6-8: cf., in one sense, *Mt.* xi, 25 = *Lk.* x, 21; pl. 81, 9-10: *Mt.* xix, 30 et xx, 16 = *Mk.* x, 31 = *Lk.* xiii, 30.

Log. 5, pl. 81, 13: *Lk.* viii, 17 (= *Mk.* iv, 22); cf. *Mt.* x, 26 = *Lk.* xii, 2.

Log. 6, pl. 81, 15-18: cf. *Mt.* vi, 1-18; pl. 81, 18: cf. *Eph.* iv, 25 and *Col.* iii, 9; pl. 81, 19: cf., in one sense, *Mt.* vii, 12 = *Lk.* vi, 31; pl. 81, 21-23: *Mt.* x, 26 = *Lk.* xii, 2 (cf. *Mk.* iv, 22 = *Lk.* viii, 17).

Log. 8, pl. 81, 29-pl. 82, 2: cf. *Mt.* xiii, 47-50; pl. 82, 2-3: *Mt.* xi, 15, xiii, 9 and 43; *Mk.* iv, 9 and 23, vii, 16; *Lk.* viii, 8, xiv, 35; *Rev.* ii, 7, xiii, 9.

Log. 9, pl. 82, 3-13: *Mt.* xiii, 3-9 = *Mk.* IV, 3-9 = *Lk.* viii, 5-8.

Log. 10, pl. 82, 14-16: cf. *Lk.* xii, 49.

Log. 11, pl. .82, 16-17: cf. *Mt.* xxiv, 35 = *Mk.* xiii, 31 = *Lk.* xxi, 33; *Mt.* v, 18 = *Lk.* xvi, 17; *I Cor.* vii, 31; *I Jn.* ii, 17.

Log. 12, pl. 82, 26-27: cf., perhaps, *Mt.* xviii, 1 = *Mk.* ix, 34 = *Lk.* ix, 46.

Log. 13, pl. 82, 30-pl. 83, 4: cf., in one sense, *Mt.* xvi, 13-16 = *Mk.* viii, 27-30 = *Lk.* ix, 18-21; pl. 83, 5: cf. *Mt.* xxiii, 8 and, perhaps, *Jn.* xv, 15; pl. 83, 6: cf. *Jn.* iv, 10-14; pl. 83, 7: cf. *Lk.* ix, 10; pl. 83, 12-13: cf. *Jn.* viii, 59 and x, 31.

Log. 14, pl. 83, 19-23: *Lk.* x, 8-9 (cf. *Mt.* x, 8; *I Cor.* x, 27); pl. 83, 24-27: *Mt.* xv, 11 = *Mk.* vii, 15.

Log. 16, pl. 83, 31- pl. 84, 3: *Lk.* xii, 49 and 51-53; cf. *Mt.* x, 34-36.

Log. 17, pl. 84, 5-9: cf. *I Cor.* ii, 9 (quoting *Is.* lxiv, 3).

Log. 19, pl. 84, 19: cf., perhaps, *Jn.* xiii, 35 and xv, 8; pl. 84, 20-21: cf., perhaps, *Mt.* iii, 9 = *Lk.* iii, 8 or *Mt.* iv, 3 = *Lk.* iv, 3; pl. 84, 21-25: cf., in one sense, *Rev.* ii, 7.

Log. 20, pl. 84, 26-33: *Mk.* iv, 30-32; cf. *Mt.* xiii, 31-32 and *Lk.* xiii, 18-19.

Log. 21, pl. 85, 4-5: cf., perhaps, *II Cor.* v, 3; pl. 85, 7-14: *Mt.* xxiv, 43-44 = *Lk.* xii, 39-40 (cf. *Mt.* vi, 19-20); pl. 85, 10: cf. *Mt.* xii, 29 = *Mk.* III, 27 = *Lk.* xi, 21-22; pl. 85, 11-12: *Lk.* xii, 35 and 37 (cf. *Mt.* xxv, 13); pl. 85, 17-18: cf. *Mk.* iv, 29 (*Joel* iii, 13); pl. 85, 19: *Mt.* xi, 15, xiii, 9 and 43; *Mk.* iv, 9 and 23, vii, 16; *Lk.* viii, 8, xiv, 35; *Rev.* ii, 7, xiii, 9.

Log. 22, pl. 85, 20-22: *Mt.* xviii, 1-3 (cf. *Mk.* ix, 36 and *Lk.* ix, 47-48); compare also *Mt.* xix, 13-15 = *Mk.* x, 13-15 = *Lk.* xviii, 15-17; pl. 85, 28-31: cf. *Gal.* iii, 28, *Eph.* ii, 14-16.

Log. 23, pl. 86, 1-2: cf. *Mt.* xxii, 14; *Jn.* vi, 70, xiii, 18, xv, 16 and 19.

Log. 24, pl. 86, 4-6: cf., perhaps, *Jn.* xiv, 4-5; pl. 86, 6-7: *Mt.* xi, 15, xiii, 9 and 43; *Mk.* iv, 9 and 23, vii, 16; *Lk.* viii, 8, xiv, 35; *Rev.* ii, 7, xiii, 9; pl. 86, 7-10: compare, perhaps, *Mt.* vi, 22-23 = *Lk.* xi, 34-35.

Log. 25, pl. 86, 10-11: *Mt.* xix, 19*b* and xxii, 39 = *Mk.* xii, 31 = *Lk.* x, 27 (= *Lev.* xix, 18, quoted also by *Jam.* ii, 8); pl. 86, 12: cf. *Deut.* xxxii, 10, *Ps.* xvii, 8, *Prov.* vii, 2, *Eccles.* xvii, 22.

Log. 26, pl. 86, 12-17: *Mt.* vii, 3-5 = *Lk.* vi, 41-42.

Log. 27, pl. 86, 18-19: cf., perhaps, *Mt.* vi, 33 = *Lk.* xii, 31; pl. 86, 20: cf. *Jn.* xiv, 9 and *Mt.* v, 8.

Log. 28, pl. 86, 22: cf. *I Tim.* iii, 16.

Log. 30, pl. 87, 3-5: cf. *Mt.* xviii, 20.

Log. 31, pl. 87, 5-7: *Mt.* xiii, 57 = *Mk.* vi, 4; *Lk.* iv, 23-24; *Jn.* iv, 44.

Log. 32, pl. 87, 8-10: *Mt.* v, 14*b*; cf. *Mt.* vii, 24-25 and *Is.* ii, 2.

Log. 33, pl. 87, 10-13: *Mt.* x, 27 = *Lk.* xii, 3; pl. 87, 13-17: *Mk.* iv, 21 = *Lk.* viii, 16; *Mt.* v, 15 = *Lk.* xi, 33.

Log. 34, pl. 87, 18-20: *Mt.* xv, 14, *Lk.* vi, 39.

Log. 35, pl. 87, 20-24: *Mt.* xii, 29 = *Mk.* iii, 27; cf. *Lk.* xi, 21-22.

Log. 36, pl. 87, 24-27: *Mt.* vi, 25 = *Lk.* xii, 22; cf. *Mt.* vi, 31 = *Lk.* xii, 29.

Log. 37, pl. 87, 27-29: cf. *Jn.* xiv, 22 and *I Jn.* iii, 2; pl. 87, 30-31: cf., in one sense, *Gen.* ii, 25 and iii, 7; pl. 88, 1: cf. *Mt.* xvi, 16.

Log. 38, pl. 88, 2-5: cf., perhaps, *Mt.* xiii, 17 = *Lk.* x, 24; pl. 88, 5-6: cf. *Mt.* ix, 15, *Mk.* ii, 20, *Lk.* v, 35 and xxi, 6; pl. 88, 6-7: cf. *Jn.* vii, 33-34 and 36.

Log. 39, pl. 88, 7-11: *Mt.* xxiii, 13 = *Lk.* xi, 52; pl. 88, 11-13: *Mt.* x, 16.

Log. 40, pl. 88, 13-16: cf. *Mt.* xv, 13 and *Jn.* xv, 1-10.

Log. 41, pl. 88, 16-18: *Mt.* xiii, 12 = *Mk.* iv, 25 = *Lk.* viii, 18; cf. *Mt.* xxv, 29 = *Lk.* xix, 26.

Log. 43, pl. 88, 20-22: cf. *Jn.* xiv, 8-11; pl. 88, 24-26: cf. *Mt.* xii, 33 = *Lk.* vi, 43-44; *Mt.* vii, 17-20.

Log. 44, pl. 88, 26-32: *Mt.* xii, 31-32 = *Mk.* iii, 28-29 = *Lk.* xii, 10.

Log. 45, pl. 88, 31-pl. 89, 5: *Lk.* vi, 44-45 = *Mt.* vii, 16 + xii, 35 + xii, 34.

Log. 46, pl. 89, 6-12: *Mt.* xi, 11 = *Lk.* vii, 28.

Log. 47, pl. 89, 14-17: *Mt.* vi, 24 = *Lk.* xvi, 13; pl. 89, 17-19: *Lk.* v, 39; pl. 89, 19-23: *Mt.* ix, 16-17 = *Mk.* ii, 21-22 = *Lk.* v, 36-38.

Log. 48, pl. 89, 24-25: *Mt.* xviii, 19 (cf., perhaps, *Mt.* xii, 25 =
Mk. iii, 25); pl. 89, 25-27: *Mt.* xvii, 20 (cf. *Mt.* xxi, 21 =
Mk. xi, 22-23). Cf. *I Cor.* xiii, 2.

Log. 50, pl. 90, 3: cf. *Lk.* xvi, 8, *Jn.* xii, 36, *Eph.* v, 8, *I Thess.* v, 5; pl.
90, 4: cf. *Jn.* vi, 57, *Rom.* ix, 26.

Log. 51, pl. 90, 11: cf., in one sense, *Mt.* xvii, 11-12, or *Jn.* v, 25.

Log. 52, pl. 90, 12-18: cf., in one sense, *Jn.* v, 39-40 and viii, 53;
moreover, *Lk.* xxiv, 5 and *Mt.* viii, 22 = *Lk.* ix, 60.

Log. 53, pl. 90, 19: cf. *Rom.* ii, 25 and iii, 1; pl. 90, 22: cf. *Rom.* ii, 29.

Log. 54, pl. 90, 23-24: *Mt.* v, 3 = *Lk.* vi, 20.

Log. 55, pl. 90, 25-29: *Mt.* x, 37-38 = *Lk.* xiv, 26-27; cf. *Mt.* xvi, 24 =
Mk. viii, 34 = *Lk.* ix, 23.

Log. 56, pl. 90, 32: cf. *Heb.* xi, 38.

Log. 57, pl. 90, 33-pl. 91, 7: *Mt.* xiii, 24-30.

Log. 58, pl. 91, 8-9: cf., in one sense, *Jam.* i, 12 and *I Pet.* iii, 14.

Log. 61, pl. 91, 23-25: *Lk.* xvii, 34 (cf. *Mt.* xxiv, 40-41); pl. 91, 29-30:
cf. *Mt.* xi, 27 = *Lk.* x, 22, *Jn.* vi, 37 and 39, xvii, 2, 6 and 9;
Lk. ii, 49.

Log. 62, pl. 92, 1-2: *Mt.* vi, 3.

Log. 63, pl. 92, 3-9: *Lk.* xii, 16-21; pl. 92, 9-10: *Mt.* xi, 15, xiii, 9 and
43; *Mk.* iv, 9 and 23, vii, 16; *Lk.* viii, 8, xiv, 35; *Rev.* ii, 7, xiii, 9.

Log. 64, pl. 92, 10-35: *Lc.* xiv, 16-24 = *Mt.* xxii, 2-10.

Log. 65, pl. 93, 1-15: *Mt.* xxi, 33-41 = *Mk.* xii, 1-8 = *Lk.* xx, 9-16;
pl. 93, 16: *Mt.* xi, 15, xiii, 9 and 43; *Mk.* iv, 9 and 23, vii,
16; *Lk.* viii, 8, xiv, 35; *Rev.* ii, 7, xiii, 9.

Log. 66, pl. 93, 16-19: *Mt.* xxi, 42 (= *Ps.* cxvii, 22) = *Mk.* xii, 10 =
Lk. xx, 17; cf. also *I Pet.* ii, 4-6.

Log. 67, pl. 93, 19-20: cf. *Mt.* xvi, 26 = *Mk.* viii, 36 = *Lk.* ix, 25.

Log. 68, pl. 93, 21-22: cf. *Mt.* v, 11 = *Lk.* vi, 22.

Log. 69, pl. 93, 25: cf. *Mt.* v, 10; pl. 93, 27: cf. *Mt.* xxii, 16, *Jn.* iv, 23
and 24, xvii, 17 and 19, etc.; pl. 93, 28: cf. *Mt.* v, 6 = *Lk.* vi, 21.

Log. 71, pl. 93, 34-35: cf., in one sense, *Mt.* xxvi, 61 (and xxvii, 40)
Mk. xiv, 58; *Jn.* ii, 19; *Acts* vi, 14.

Log. 72, pl. 94, 1-6: *Lk.* xii, 13-14.

Log. 73, pl. 94, 6-9: *Mt.* ix, 37-38 = *Lk.* x, 2.

Log. 75, pl. 94, 11-13: cf., perhaps, *Mt.* xxii, 10-14, ix, 15 (= *Mk.* ii,
19 = *Lk.* v, 34; cf. *Jn.* iii, 29) and xxv, 10.

Log. 76, pl. 94, 14-19: *Mt.* xiii, 45-46; pl. 94, 19-20: cf. *Mt.* xiii, 44;
pl. 94, 19-22: *Mt.* vi, 19-20 = *Lk.* xii, 33.

Log. 77, pl. 94, 23: cf. *Jn.* viii, 12; pl. 94, 25-26: cf. *Rom.* xi, 36, and
I Cor. viii, 6.

Log. 78, pl. 94, 28-pl. 95, 2: *Mt.* xi, 7-8 = *Lk.* vii, 24-25; pl. 94, 32:
Rev. vi, 15 (cf. *Ps.* ii, 2, *Is.* xxiv, 21) and *Mt.* xx, 25.

Log. 79, pl. 95, 3-8: *Lk.* xi, 27-28; pl. 95, 9-12: *Lk.* xxiii, 29. Cf. also *Mt.* xxiv, 19 = *Mk.* xiii, 17 = *Lk.* xxi, 23.

Log. 81, pl. 95, 15-16: cf. *I Cor.* iv, 8.

Log. 82, pl. 95, 17-19: cf., in one sense, *Mk.* xii, 34.

Log. 86, pl. 95, 34-pl. 96, 4: *Mt.* viii, 20 = *Lk.* ix, 58.

Log. 88, pl. 96, 7-9: cf. *Mt.* xvi, 27 = *Mk.* viii, 38*b* = *Lk.* ix, 26*b*.

Log. 89, pl. 96, 13-16: *Mt.* xxiii, 26 = *Lk.* xi, 39-40.

Log. 90, pl. 96, 17-19: *Mt.* xi, 28-30.

Log. 91, pl. 96, 21: cf. *Jn.* vi, 30; pl. 96, 22-25: *Lk.* xii, 56 = *Mt.* xvi, 3.

Log. 92, pl. 96, 26: cf., in one sense, *Mt.* vii, 7-8 = *Lk.* xi, 9-10.

Log. 93, pl. 96, 30-33: *Mt.* vii, 6.

Log. 94, pl. 96, 33-34: *Mt.* vii, 8 = *Lk.* xi, 10.

Log. 95, pl. 96, 35-pl. 97, 2: *Lk.* vi, 34-35 (cf. vi, 30 and *Mt.* v, 42).

Log. 96, pl. 97, 2-5: *Mt.* xiii, 33 = *Lk.* xiii, 20-21; pl. 97, 6: *Mt.* xi, 15, xiii, 9 and 43; *Mk.* iv, 9 and 23, vii, 16; *Lk.* viii, 8, xiv, 35; *Rev.* ii, 7, xiii, 9.

Log. 99, pl. 97, 21-26: *Mt.* xii, 47-50 = *Mk.* iii, 32-35 = *Lk.* viii, 20-21.

Log. 100, pl. 97, 27-30: *Mt.* xxii, 16-21 = *Mk.* xii, 13-17 = *Lk.* xx, 21-25.

Log. 101, pl. 97, 32-33: *Mt.* x, 37 = *Lk.* xiv, 26; cf. *Mt.* xix, 29 = *Mk.* x, 29 = *Lk.* xviii, 29*b*.

Log. 102, pl. 98, 2: cf. *Lk.* xi, 42 and 43, *Mt.* xxiii, 13, 14, 15, 23, 25, 27 and 29.

Log. 103, pl. 98, 6-8: cf. *Mt.* xxiv, 43 = *Lk.* xii, 39; pl. 98, 9-10: cf. *Lk.* xii, 35.

Log. 104, pl. 98, 10-16: *Mt.* ix, 14-15 = *Mk.* ii, 18-20 = *Lk.* v, 33-35.

Log. 105, pl. 98, 17-18: cf., perhaps, *Jn.* viii, 41.

Log. 107, pl. 98, 22-27: *Mt.* xviii, 12-13 = *Lk.* xv, 3-6.

Log. 108, pl. 98, 28-29: cf., in one sense, *Jn.* vii, 37.

Log. 109, pl. 98, 31-pl. 99, 3: cf. *Mt.* xiii, 44.

Log. 111, pl. 99, 6: cf. *Is.* xxxiv, 4, *Heb.* i, 12, *Rev.* vi, 14.

Log. 113, pl. 99, 12-18: *Lk.* xvii, 20-21; cf., perhaps, *Mt.* xxiv, 23 and *Jn.* i, 26.

GARY LIBRARY